EVERYONE CAN BAKE

SIMPLE RECIPES TO MASTER AND MIX

DOMINIQUE ANSEL

PHOTOGRAPHS BY EVAN SUNG

SIMON & SCHUSTER

NEW YORK   LONDON   TORONTO   SYDNEY   NEW DELHI

Simon & Schuster
1230 Avenue of the Americas
New York, NY 10020

First Simon & Schuster hardcover edition April 2020

SIMON & SCHUSTER and colophon are registered trademarks of Simon & Schuster, Inc.

For information about special discounts for bulk purchases, please contact Simon & Schuster Special Sales at 1-866-506-1949 or business@simonandschuster.com.

The Simon & Schuster Speakers Bureau can bring authors to your live event. For more information or to book an event, contact the Simon & Schuster Speakers Bureau at 1-866-248-3049 or visit our website at www.simonspeakers.com.

Interior design by Suet Yee Chong

Manufactured in China

10 9 8 7 6 5 4 3 2 1

Library of Congress Cataloging-in-Publication Data is available.

ISBN 978-1-5011-9471-9
ISBN 978-1-5011-9472-6 (ebook)

To A, because no one does it alone

CONTENTS

FINISHINGS 212

ASSEMBLY & TECHNIQUES 281

	BASE	FILLING	FINISHING	TECHNIQUE
TARTS				
Mixed Fruit Tart	Vanilla Sablé Tart Shell (page 4)	Pastry Cream (page 121)	Assorted fresh fruits (page 248)	How to Build a Tart (page 286)
Baked Apple Almond Frangipane Tart	Sablé Breton (page 91)	Almond Frangipane (page 123)	Caramelized Apples (page 240)	Baked Almond Frangipane Tart (page 93)
Flan	Vanilla Sablé Tart Shell (page 4)	Pastry Cream (page 121)		Flan (page 10)
Lemon Earl Grey Tart	Hazelnut Sablé Tart Shell (page 15)	Lemon Curd (page 134)	Earl Grey Italian Meringue (page 261)	How to Build a Tart (page 286)
Strawberry Honey Crème Fraîche Tart	Vanilla Sablé Tart Shell (page 4)	Pastry Cream (page 121) + Crème Fraîche Whipped Ganache (page 184) + Strawberry Jam (page 159)	Fresh strawberries, honeycomb, Nappage Glaze (page 223)	How to Build a Tart (page 286)
Cherry Tart	Vanilla Sablé Tart Shell (page 4)	Cherry Jam (page 163) + Almond Cake (page 34) + Pastry Cream (page 121)	Nappage Glaze (page 223) + fresh cherries	How to Build a Tart (page 286)
Salted Caramel Chocolate Tart	Chocolate Sablé Tart Shell (page 12)	Dark Chocolate Ganache (page 137)	Caramel Glaze (page 227) + sea salt	How to Build a Tart (page 286)
CAKES				
Lemon Pound Cake	Lemon Pound Cake (page 72)		Nappage Glaze (page 223)	

	BASE	FILLING	FINISHING	TECHNIQUE
CAKES				
Banana Bread with Chestnut-Whiskey Chantilly Cream	Banana Bread (page 60)		Caramelized Bananas (page 238) + Chestnut-Whiskey Chantilly Cream (page 253)	
Tiramisu	Ladyfingers (page 46) + Amaretto Espresso Syrup (page 29)	Mascarpone Whipped Ganache (page 178)	Cocoa powder	Tiramisu (page 53)
Triple Chocolate Cake	Chocolate Cake (page 22)	Dark Chocolate Ganache (page 137)	Chocolate Buttercream (page 222) + cocoa powder	How to Assemble a Layer Cake (page 293)
Chocolate Cherry Cake	Brownie Base (page 84)	Cherry Jam (page 163)	Chocolate Buttercream (page 222) + fresh cherries	How to Assemble a Layer Cake (page 293)
Apricot Elderflower Roulade	Almond Cake (page 34) + Elderflower Syrup (page 30)	Vanilla Whipped Ganache (page 187) + Apricot Gelée (page 168)	Fresh apricots + Nappage Glaze (page 223)	Roulade (page 36)
Peach Muscovado Sugar Charlotte	Ladyfingers (page 46) + Rose Water Syrup (page 29)	Strawberry Jam (page 159) + Muscovado Sugar Whipped Ganache (page 186) + fresh peaches	Nappage Glaze (page 223)	Charlotte (page 56)
Fig Molasses Olive Oil Cake	Molasses Almond Cake (page 39)	Olive Oil Mousse (page 196) + Fig Jam (page 162)	Fresh figs + Vanilla Chantilly Cream (page 252)	How to Assemble a Mousse Cake (page 299)
Chocolate Chip Cookie Coconut Cake	Cookie Base (page 76) + Chocolate Cake (page 22)	Coconut Whipped Ganache (page 181)	Italian Meringue (page 258)	How to Assemble a Layer Cake (page 293)

	BASE	FILLING	FINISHING	TECHNIQUE
MOUSSE CAKES AND MORE				
Hazelnut Chocolate Cherry Cake	Cherry Chocolate Cake (page 26)	Milk Chocolate Mousse (page 204, made with gianduja)	Dark Chocolate Glaze (page 230)	How to Assemble a Mousse Cake (page 299)
Peanut Butter Crunch Cake	Caramelized Puffed Rice Base (page 100)	Peanut Butter Mousse (page 195)	Dark Chocolate Ganache (page 137)	How to Assemble a Mousse Cake (page 299)
Matcha Passion Fruit Mousse Cake	Almond Cake (page 34)	Matcha Mousse (page 192) + Passion Fruit Curd (page 136)	White Chocolate Glaze (page 234)	How to Assemble a Mousse Cake (page 299)
Chocolate Champagne Pear Cake	Chocolate Cake (page 22)	Dark Chocolate Champagne Mousse (page 204) + Pear Compote (page 151)	Caramelized Pears (page 241) + Chocolate Buttercream (page 222)	How to Assemble a Mousse Cake (page 299)
Raspberry Cream Puff Cake	Round Choux Base, with Profiterole Top (page 112)	Raspberry Jam (page 159)	Fresh raspberries + Vanilla Chantilly Cream (page 252)	
Grapefruit Tarragon Pavlova	Italian Meringue (Baked) (page 258)	Grapefruit Curd (page 136)	Fresh grapefruit + Tarragon Chantilly Cream (page 253) + Nappage Glaze (page 223)	
Blackberry Lemon Verbena Pavlova	Italian Meringue (Baked) (page 258)	Blackberry Jam (page 159) + Lemon Verbena Chiboust (page 127)	Fresh blackberries	

	BASE	FILLING	FINISHING	TECHNIQUE
SOMETHING SWEET				
Chocolate Chip Cookie	Chocolate Chip Cookie (page 80)			
Chocolate Chip Ice Cream Sandwich	Chocolate Chip Cookie (page 80)		Vanilla Ice Cream (page 274)	
Linzer Cookie	Gingerbread Sablé Tart Shell (page 14)	Raspberry Jam (page 159)	Confectioners' sugar	Linzer Cookie (page 7)
Basil Truffles		Basil Dark Chocolate Ganache (page 142)	Cocoa powder	Truffles (page 140)
Chocolate Mousse		Milk Chocolate Mousse (page 204)	Vanilla Chantilly Cream (page 252)	
Roasted Fruit Crumble			Roasted Fruit (page 246) + Streusel Crumble (page 268)	
Rosemary Caramel Brownie	Rosemary-Infused Chocolate Brownies (page 88)	Soft Caramel (page 208)	Sea salt	
Hazelnut Meringues + Ice Cream			Ice Cream (page 274) + Toasted Hazelnut Meringue (page 265)	

The Building Blocks of Baking

When I was growing up, I loved to play with building blocks. With the blocks scattered across the floor of my parents' living room, I saw endless possibilities: each cube could become something new and different when joined with another.

I never got tired of playing that game. These days, in the kitchen, I still play the role of builder and architect. A chef, unlike a home cook, doesn't follow a recipe for a cake, with a prescribed base, filling, and finishing. We share basic recipes for *components*, and build those into cookies, cakes, tarts, and other showstoppers.

These components are the building blocks of baking. And with them, there are endless dessert possibilities.

This is the way I want to teach you how to bake.

The book is split into three sections:

> **BASES:** cakes, tarts, cookies, brownies, and more

> **FILLINGS:** mousses, jams, curds, pastry creams, and more

> **FINISHINGS:** meringues, chocolate glazes, and more

Each recipe starts off with a reliable go-to—this is your baseline. Perfect these first, then explore their variations. A vanilla cake with a bit of clove, ginger, and cinnamon turns into a wonderful gingerbread for the holidays. A pastry cream can be mixed with fruit or chocolate or even hazelnut paste.

Select from each of the three sections to create your showstopper. Choose a base, a filling, and a finishing, then combine them. And don't worry—I'll show you how to do that in the Techniques section where you assemble everything together. Perhaps you're in the mood for a decadent cake with a brownie base, a rich mascarpone mousse filling, and a caramel glaze. Or maybe a light lemon tart with a vanilla meringue.

Many of these components can be enjoyed on their own, and I'll show you how to do that, too. A ganache can be chilled and rolled into chocolate truffles. A pastry cream can become a makeshift flan. A tart shell can be broken and sandwiched together with jam to make a cookie.

You'll learn to bake, but more important, to create. The possibilities really are endless.

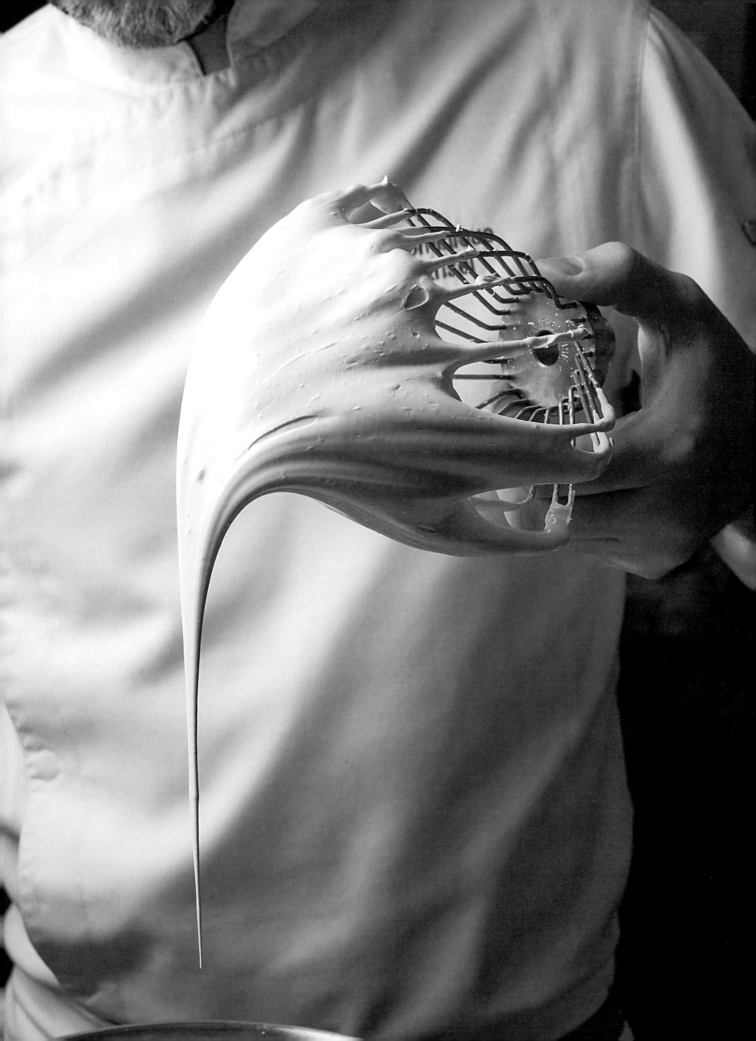

WHAT TOOLS SHOULD YOU BUY?

There's a precision to baking that's always appealed to me. I love that there were exact metrics and temperatures; nothing is left up to chance. But it's that precision that is perhaps the biggest hurdle for a lot of home cooks to overcome. Investing in the right tools is a big help here. In baking, "a pinch of this" and a "dash of that" could throw off the entire recipe. (Have you ever mistakenly measured a tablespoon of baking powder instead of a teaspoon? I'm sure it was a disaster you won't forget.) Each ingredient is precisely measured on a scale. And there's the right set of equipment for each task.

Here are the tools I recommend for cooking your way through this book, from the Bare Necessities that you need for making a simple cookie or brownie to the Standard Additions for making cakes and tarts to the Upgrades I recommend for making even more advanced recipes.

BARE NECESSITIES

Bowls (various sizes)

Cutting board

Digital scale

Knives (small paring knife, large chef's knife, and large serrated knife)

Parchment paper

Rolling pin

Saucepans (various sizes)

Sheet pan

Spatula (heatproof)

Whisk

Wire rack

STANDARD ADDITIONS

Bowl scraper

Cake pan and cake ring (8-inch or 20 cm round)

Loaf pan (8½ x 4½ inch or 21 x 11 cm)

Hand mixer

Offset spatulas (large and small)

Piping bags

Fine-mesh sieve

Silicone baking mat

Tart ring (8-inch or 20 cm)

UPGRADES

Digital thermometer

Pastry brush

Rotating cake stand

Silicone cake molds

Stand mixer

TIMING

Baking isn't instantaneous in the same way that cooking can be. You can fry up an egg or boil some pasta in minutes, but baking is a slower game. That's why it's often done as a hobby or group event—it requires you to spend time on it. While the steps themselves do not always take a while, they sometimes demand a practice of patience. You wait for the dough to chill before rolling it out. You wait for the cake to bake. You wait for the jam to cool or the mousse to thaw. Here are some quick guidelines for how much time you should set aside, depending on what you're baking.

Set aside an hour or so for any batter-based recipe that doesn't require additional components for assembly, such as:

> Cookies

> Brownies

> Loaf cakes

Set aside a morning or an afternoon for any recipe that has multiple components and requires assembly, like:

> Tarts

> Standard cakes

Plan on waiting overnight before you can enjoy any recipe that requires freezing or extended baking times, such as:

> Mousse cake

> Pavlova

If you're like me, you like to plan ahead. Here are some guidelines for what you can and cannot do beforehand.

CAN DO BEFORE

> Tart and cookie doughs can be prepared and refrigerated for 1 to 2 days before baking.

> Pastry creams, curds, jams, and ganaches can be prepared and refrigerated for up to 3 days, then used to fill a cake or tart the day of.

> Glazes can be prepared and refrigerated for up to 7 days, then reheated the day of.

CANNOT DO BEFORE

> Batters must be baked immediately, as not to deflate or separate.

> Anything whipped must be whipped and used within a few minutes, or it will lose volume.

Once you've planned your time and set yourself up for success with the right tools—it's time for the fun to begin.

Turn the page for some ideas to get started.

BASES

Here we are at the start—for a baker, choosing a base is the first step in your creative adventure. So first, you must decide what you want: A tart for Sunday lunch? A cake for a birthday celebration? Or a batch of brownies for an afternoon snack? Once you decide on the base, you can map out what comes next.

What I love the most about this choice is that it's often not about *just* you. I would guess that you're often baking for someone else, and thinking about what they would like, too—for their lunch, birthday, their snack. That's what makes baking so special. You need your hands to follow the recipes and techniques, but you need your heart to bake.

Where do you want to go? What is your heart's desire?

MY GO-TO VANILLA SABLÉ TART SHELL

A proper tart shell should be golden brown, uniformly thin, crispy, and have smooth, clean edges. When you bite into it, it should melt in your mouth as you chew. I'm practical when it comes to tart shells. To me, a tart shell must serve a purpose: it should carry as much fresh fruit as possible. During the summer in France, this means a punnet of ripe woodland strawberries—they taste so sweet, they could be candy—arranged on top of a layer of whipped vanilla ganache. I add as many as I can, so there's not a sliver of ganache visible. A little strawberry jam piped on top deepens the tart's flavor.

MAKES: One 8-inch (20 cm) tart shell
TIME: 1 hour (including time to blind bake)

INGREDIENTS

185 grams	1½ cups	all-purpose flour, plus more for dusting
85 grams	⅔ cup	confectioners' sugar
50 grams	5¼ tablespoons	cornstarch
1 gram	¼ teaspoon	Kosher salt
3 grams	½	Tahitian vanilla bean, split lengthwise, seeds scraped
130 grams	10 tablespoons (1¼ sticks)	unsalted butter, cut into cubes, at room temperature
50 grams	1 large	egg

EQUIPMENT
8-inch (20 cm) tart ring or pan

1. Make the dough: Combine the flour, confectioners' sugar, cornstarch, salt, and vanilla seeds in a large bowl. Add the butter and mix with your hands until the butter is broken down into pieces the size of peas and the ingredients are well combined. (Alternatively, use a stand mixer or hand mixer to combine the ingredients.) Add the egg and mix with a spatula until the dough is smooth and the egg is fully incorporated. Don't overmix.

2. Chill the dough: Turn the dough out onto a large piece of plastic wrap and gently shape it into a ball. Wrap the dough in the plastic wrap and flatten it into a disc. Refrigerate for at least 30 minutes or up to overnight, until cold but still pliable. It should have the texture of clay.* (At this point, the dough can be refrigerated or frozen for later use—see Storage.)

  * *Flattening the dough into a disc will help it chill faster. You'll want to make sure the dough is cold before rolling it out. Working with dough that's too warm will cause the tart shell to shrink as it bakes.*

3. Preheat the oven: Place a rack in the center of the oven and preheat the oven to 350°F (175°C).

4. Roll out the dough: Flour your work surface and rolling pin. Unwrap the dough and place it on your work surface. Roll it out into a rectangle about ⅛ inch (3 mm) thick.* Make sure to work quickly so the dough doesn't get too warm.

  * *If you find that your dough is sticking to the rolling pin or work surface, add some more flour. Then roll it out between two sheets of parchment paper. Parchment paper also makes it easier to lift the rolled-out dough onto the sheet pan later on.*

5. Shape the dough: Using an 8-inch (20 cm) tart ring or pan as a guide, cut the dough into a round that's 1 inch (2.5 cm) wider than the ring (this ensures the dough will come up the sides of the tart ring).*

  * *Don't throw out your dough scraps! Sprinkle them with cinnamon sugar (I make mine with 3 grams (1 teaspoon) of cinnamon to 100 grams (½ cup) of granulated sugar) and bake them, then enjoy them as buttery sugar cookies or crumbled over your morning yogurt.*

6. Now the fun part: you're going to **"fonçage"** the tart dough (page 282), or form it into a tart shape. (Don't worry, it's not as intimidating as it sounds!) Butter the tart ring or pan. If you're using a tart ring, line a sheet pan with parchment paper, then set the tart ring in the center (no need to do this if you're using a tart pan with a bottom). Place the round of dough on top of the tart ring or pan and push down gently with your fingers, pressing the dough along the inside of the ring or pan and into the inside edge. Don't press too hard, and try to keep the dough an even thickness so that it bakes evenly. Use a paring knife to trim any dough hanging over the sides of the ring or pan.*

  * *If your dough is starting to feel warm, return it to the refrigerator for 15 minutes before baking. Remember, warm or overworked dough will shrink as it bakes. If the dough is cool to the touch, you can bake it right away.*

7. Blind bake the tart shell*: Line the tart shell with a round of parchment or a large coffee filter; the surface of the dough should be completely covered.* Fill the tart shell with uncooked rice or dried beans to keep the dough in place. Bake on the center rack until the tart shell is light golden brown, 15 to 20 minutes.

  * *Since many tarts are filled with creams or mousses (which aren't baked), you'll have to bake the tart shell in advance of filling it. This is called blind baking. If you're planning to fill your tart shell with Almond Frangipane (page 123), however, DO NOT blind bake the*

tart shell first. The almond frangipane contains raw eggs, so it needs to be baked, too. Pipe the almond frangipane into an unbaked tart shell first and then bake.

* *Here's an easy trick to cut a perfect circle: Fold a square of parchment paper in half, then in half again. Fold it in half diagonally to form a triangle, then fold the triangle in half once more. Flip your pan upside down and place the folded paper triangle with the narrow tip at the center of the pan. Using scissors, cut the base of the triangle (the side opposite the tip) into a curve, following the curve of the pan. Unfold the paper: it should now be a circle slightly larger than the tart ring or pan.*

8. Unmold the tart shell: Cool for 2 to 3 minutes, then unmold the tart shell while still warm (it's easier to remove from the pan when it's warm). If you're using a tart pan with a removable bottom, set the pan on an upside-down pint container or a small bowl and push down gently on the sides of the pan to unmold the tart shell. If you're using a tart ring, lift the ring up and off the tart shell. Let cool completely before filling.* Wait until just before serving to add the filling so the shell stays nice and crispy.

* *Before you start assembling a cream-filled tart, always make sure the tart shell is fully cooled. If the shell is too hot, the pastry cream will melt and soak into the crust, giving you a soggy-bottomed tart.*

STORAGE

The tart shell is best enjoyed the day it's baked, but can be stored in an airtight container in a cool, dry place for up to 2 days before filling and serving.

The unbaked tart dough can be wrapped tightly in plastic wrap and stored in the refrigerator for up to 3 days or in the freezer for 2 to 3 weeks. Thaw the frozen dough in the refrigerator for a few hours before using.

PAIR IT WITH

> **RECOMMENDED FILLINGS:** pastry cream, lemon curd, jam, compote, ganache, whipped ganache

> **RECOMMENDED FINISHINGS:** meringue, fresh fruit, Chantilly cream, streusel

TWO IDEAS TO GET YOU STARTED

> Lemon Curd (page 134) with Italian Meringue (page 258)

> Vanilla Whipped Ganache (page 187) with fresh strawberries (page 248)

LINZER COOKIES

Roll the dough slightly thicker than a tart shell, ¼ inch (6 mm) thick. Use your favorite cookie cutter to cut shapes from the dough. With a smaller cookie cutter, cut a smaller shape from the center of half the cookies. Arrange all the cookies on a parchment paper–lined sheet pan and bake in a preheated 350°F (175°C) oven for 10 minutes. Let cool completely in the pan. Turn the cookies without the center hole bottom-side up and dollop a teaspoon of your favorite jam (the classic choice is Raspberry Jam, page 159) onto each. Dust the cookies with the center hole with confectioners' sugar and place on top of the jam. Push down slightly to make a sandwich. Once assembled, the cookies can be stored in an airtight container in a cool, dry place for up to 2 days.

LINZER COOKIES
BASE: Gingerbread Sablé Tart Shell (page 14)
FILLING: Raspberry Jam (page 159)
FINISHING: Confectioners' sugar
TECHNIQUE: Linzer Cookie (page 7)

FLAN

A flan is a two component dessert that doesn't need much else. Simply get a taller cake pan to line your Go-To Vanilla Sablé Tart Shell (page 4). I like a 3-inch tall (6.75 cm) and 8-inch wide (20 cm) pan. Then prepare your Go-To Pastry Cream recipe (page 121). While the pastry cream is still warm (but not piping hot), pour it into the tart shell. Bake at 350°F (175°C) until the flan is dark brown on top, 25 to 30 minutes. Let cool completely before unmolding and serving. Once baked, it can be kept refrigerated for 2 days.

FLAN
BASE: Vanilla Sablé Tart Shell (page 4)
FILLING: Pastry Cream (page 121)
TECHNIQUE: Flan (page 10)

CHOCOLATE SABLÉ TART SHELL

BASE

MY GO-TO VANILLA SABLÉ TART SHELL

Adding cocoa powder to my vanilla sablé tart shell results in a rich chocolate shell that can turn a classic tart into something a bit more decadent. This variation works well with fruit fillings like fresh berries (page 248) or Caramelized Bananas (page 238), or with even more chocolate like a smooth chocolate ganache (page 137) or a light and airy chocolate mousse (page 204).

THE CHANGE

In step 1 of **My Go-To Vanilla Sablé Tart Shell** (page 4), add **18 grams (2½ tablespoons) unsweetened cocoa powder** to the dry ingredients before adding the butter, then proceed with the recipe as directed. The dark color of the dough makes it hard to tell when the chocolate tart shell is done baking. To avoid overbaking, check the tart a minute or so early; if there are no wet spots, it's ready.

TWO IDEAS TO GET YOU STARTED

> Soft Caramel (page 208) with Caramelized Bananas (page 238)
> Cherry Jam (page 163) with Vanilla Chantilly Cream (page 252)

SHOWSTOPPER

SALTED CARAMEL CHOCOLATE TART (page 13): Chocolate Sablé Tart Shell (above) filled with Dark Chocolate Ganache (page 137) and finished with Caramel Glaze (page 227) and a sprinkling of sea salt

SALTED CARAMEL CHOCOLATE TART

BASE: Chocolate Sablé Tart Shell (page 12)
FILLING: Dark Chocolate Ganache (page 137)
FINISHING: Caramel Glaze (page 227)
TECHNIQUE: How to Build a Tart (page 286)

GINGERBREAD SABLÉ TART SHELL

Brown sugar, cinnamon, and ground ginger subtly spice this variation. The tart shell has rich, caramel color and flavor, thanks to the molasses in the brown sugar and the warm spices. Pair it with apples and pears for winter holidays.

THE CHANGE

In step 1 of **My Go-To Vanilla Sablé Tart Shell** (page 4), replace the confectioners' sugar with **85 grams (½ cup) dark brown sugar**, and add **4 grams (1½ teaspoons) ground cinnamon** and **4 grams (1½ teaspoons) ground ginger*** to the dry ingredients before adding the butter. Proceed with the recipe as directed.

> * *I like to use ground ginger rather than fresh in this tart shell because the intensity of fresh ginger can vary, which can easily make your recipe either too spicy or too mild.*

TWO IDEAS TO GET YOU STARTED

> Muscovado Sugar Whipped Ganache (page 186) with Streusel Crumble (page 268)

> Mascarpone Whipped Ganache (page 178) with Apple Compote (page 150)

HAZELNUT SABLÉ TART SHELL

I've always loved hazelnuts. I think it's because I used to eat Nutella straight out of the jar when I was a kid, and that memory has stayed with me all these years. Here I've substituted some of the all-purpose flour in my vanilla tart shell with hazelnut flour, which gives the tart shell a nutty flavor and crumblier texture. It works well with a rich chocolate ganache filling or a tart, creamy orange curd.

THE CHANGE

In step 1 of **My Go-To Vanilla Sablé Tart Shell** (page 4), reduce the all-purpose flour to 125 grams (1 cup) and add **60 grams (½ cup) hazelnut flour**. Since hazelnut flour contains no gluten, the dough for this tart shell will be crumblier, so handle it delicately. Proceed with the recipe as directed.

TWO IDEAS TO GET YOU STARTED

> Orange Curd (page 136) with Toasted Hazelnut Meringue (page 265)
> Raspberry Chocolate Ganache (page 143)

SHOWSTOPPER

LEMON EARL GREY TART: Hazelnut Sablé Tart Shell (above) filled with Lemon Curd (page 134) and finished with Earl Grey Italian Meringue (page 261)

Everyone Can Bake

Over the years, I've heard the proclamation many times, in many different ways. But I had never challenged it . . . until now.

Over dinner one night, a friend loudly said, "I can cook, but baking? I'm too scared to do that." It was the word "scared" that got me. I've not often heard anyone say they're *scared* of cooking. What about baking caused so much extra fear and distress?

I needed an answer.

I started asking people about the first dish they ever made. The answers were practically unanimous. It was never grilling a piece of steak or poaching a fillet of fish. It was very rarely even boiling water for a simple bowl of pasta. Almost always it was something they had baked. Chocolate chip cookies coming out of the oven, banana bread unmolded from a loaf pan, a vanilla birthday cake iced for someone special. For so many people, myself included, our earliest memories of being in the kitchen involve the oven. Leveling off flour in measuring cups. Mixing batter with a wooden spoon, then licking the bowl at the end. I remember the first time I cracked an egg—that satisfying crunch of the shell as it smacked against the side of the bowl, and how careful I was to not have a chipped shell drop into the bowl.

Somewhere between these special moments as kids and our days as adults, something changed. While our fearless young minds once ventured into baking with excitement, our adult minds approach it with unease. What burned us? A collapsed soufflé, a lumpy custard, a melted mousse? When did we outgrow baking?

One day, long after that fateful dinner, I was observing a kids' baking class. A young girl was about to make a horrible mistake by cracking her eggs directly into a pan of hot cream, which would have caused the mixture to scramble. A hand reached out to stop her and showed her how to slowly add the cream to the yolks to temper them. That's when it hit me: A parent was the missing piece. A parent who purchased the ingredients, gathered the tools, and made sure to remind us to check the oven so our cake didn't burn. Without that safety net, we got lazy. What used to be a pastime became a chore, now that we had to do the backend work. So people started winging it. When they didn't have proper ingredients, they made substitutions. Without the right measuring tools (please, consider this another plea to invest in a scale!), they started eyeballing the measurements. People didn't outgrow baking—they never grew up and accepted the responsibilities of the task.

The instructions are precise. Specific measurements, set temperatures—no mention of "season to taste" or "a sprinkle of this," "a splash of that." Baking is a discipline in the sense that it is exacting. You have to build the right foundations and learn the techniques. Understand the rules before you twist them. Innovation comes after perfecting the fundamentals.

After months of coaxing, I convinced my friend to bake. The right way—with proper preparation and a setup for success. I stepped in as a parent would, reminding her what to pay attention to during the crucial moments. "It's not as stressful as I thought," she said, after placing her sheet pan in the oven. She squinted and stared through the oven window as she waited, just as giddy and impatient as she had been as a child, and said, "I wonder when these will be done." Some things never change. And the room filled with the smell of cookies.

CHOCOLATE CHIP COOKIE
BASE: Chocolate Chip Cookie Base (page 80)

MY GO-TO CHOCOLATE CAKE

When it comes to chocolate, I believe more is more: sandwich this decadent base with a filling of chocolate ganache, or top it with chocolate mousse and cover it with a chocolate glaze.

MAKES: One 8-inch (20 cm) cake (2 to 2½ inches or 5 to 6.25 cm tall)
TIME: 1 hour 30 minutes

INGREDIENTS

220 grams	1⅓ cups	all-purpose flour, plus more for dusting
300 grams	1½ cups	granulated sugar
45 grams	½ cup	unsweetened cocoa powder (not Dutch-process)
2 grams	½ teaspoon	baking powder
3 grams	½ teaspoon	baking soda
1 gram	¼ teaspoon	salt
90 grams	2 large	eggs*
115 grams	⅔ cup	vegetable oil
225 grams	1 cup	whole milk

> * If a recipe calls for eggs in grams and you don't have a scale handy, remember the "30-20-10" rule. A large egg in the shell generally weighs about 60 grams: the white is 30 grams, the yolk is 20 grams, the shell is 10 grams. You can use those numbers to figure out how many eggs you'll need.

EQUIPMENT

8-inch (20 cm) round cake pan

1. Preheat the oven: Preheat the oven to 350°F (175°C). Butter the bottom, sides, and edges of an 8-inch (20 cm) round cake pan. Pour in some flour* and shake it around until the pan is evenly coated, then tap out any excess flour.

> * If you don't plan on frosting your chocolate cake, use cocoa powder instead of flour to dust the pan. That way when you unmold the cake, you won't see any spots of white flour on the surface.

2. Combine the dry ingredients: Whisk together the flour, sugar, cocoa powder, baking powder, baking soda, and salt in a large bowl until combined.*

> * You don't need to sift the dry ingredients; whisking them gets rid of any lumps.

3. Combine the wet ingredients: Whisk together the eggs, vegetable oil, and milk in a medium bowl until combined.

4. Make the batter: Add the wet ingredients to the dry ingredients in thirds, mixing with a spatula until combined after each addition. You should now have a velvety smooth chocolate batter. (If you spot any lumps, use a whisk to break them up, then mix the batter a bit more.)

5. Bake the cake: Pour the batter into the prepared pan until it reaches halfway up the sides. Level the surface with a spatula. Bake until the cake is set in the center, 45 to 50 minutes. It can be hard to tell if a chocolate cake is cooked through because of its dark color, and since oven temperatures can vary, you shouldn't rely solely on your timer. There are three ways to check if it's done:

> *Jiggle it:* The cake should wiggle a little in the middle. If it wiggles a lot, it's not ready.

> *Nudge it:* Press the top gently; it should bounce back to your touch.

> *Poke it:* Stick a toothpick or paring knife into the center of the cake. If it comes out clean, it's done.

6. Cool and unmold the cake: Let the cake cool in the pan for 15 minutes. While the cake is still warm, place a large plate over it, then flip the plate and pan together; the cake should easily slide out of the pan onto the plate.*

* *To make sure the cake unmolds cleanly and easily from the pan, remember three things:*
  * *Always properly butter the pan and dust it with flour (or cocoa powder) before adding the batter.*
  * *Let the cake cool for a bit once it's out of the oven, but don't wait until it has cooled completely to turn it out of the pan—it's best to unmold it while it's still a bit warm so it doesn't stick to the pan.*
  * *If the cake does stick, run a paring knife along the side of the pan to help coax it out.*

STORAGE

The cake is best enjoyed the same day it's baked, but can be wrapped tightly with plastic wrap and refrigerated for up to 3 days. For longer storage, wrap it tightly with plastic wrap, place in an airtight container, and freeze for up to 3 weeks. To use a frozen cake, remove it from the airtight container and transfer it to the refrigerator (still in the plastic wrap) to thaw for at least 3 hours or up to overnight, until the cake is soft again.

PAIR IT WITH

> **RECOMMENDED FILLINGS:** curd, jam, gelée, compote, ganache, mousse, whipped ganache

> **RECOMMENDED FINISHINGS:** buttercream, Italian meringue, glaze, Chantilly cream, streusel crumble

TWO IDEAS TO GET YOU STARTED

> One layer: Dark Chocolate Ganache (page 137)

> Two layers: Passion Fruit Curd (page 136) with Chocolate Buttercream (page 222)

SHOWSTOPPER

TRIPLE CHOCOLATE CAKE (page 292): Chocolate Cake (page 22) filled with Dark Chocolate Ganache (page 137) and finished with Chocolate Buttercream (page 222) and cocoa powder

CHOCOLATE CHAMPAGNE PEAR CAKE (page 202): Chocolate Cake (page 22) filled with Dark Chocolate Champagne Mousse (page 204), finished with fresh or Caramelized Pears (page 241)

CHOCOLATE BOURBON CAKE

BASE

MY GO-TO
CHOCOLATE CAKE

For a grown-up chocolate cake, modify My Go-To Chocolate Cake by adding a splash of your favorite bourbon. Adding alcohol to cakes imparts flavor and moisture for an even more decadent taste and texture.

THE CHANGE

In step 4 of **My Go-To Chocolate Cake** (page 22), whisk the wet ingredients into the dry ingredients as directed, then whisk in **100 grams (4 ounces) bourbon**.* Proceed as directed in the recipe, noting that the added liquid in the batter means the cake will take a few minutes longer to bake.

> * *You can use whiskey or rum instead of bourbon in this variation. What types of alcohol don't work? White wine and Champagne—because they're lighter and less concentrated, you wouldn't taste them in a dark, rich chocolate batter.*

TWO IDEAS TO GET YOU STARTED

> One layer: Peanut Butter Mousse (page 195)
> Two layers: Spiked Dark Chocolate Ganache (page 144, with bourbon) with Vanilla Chantilly Cream (page 252)

CHERRY CHOCOLATE CAKE

BASE

MY GO-TO
CHOCOLATE CAKE

Folding fresh fruit into the batter for chocolate cake gives it a burst of flavor. The key is to select fruit that is firm and not too juicy. Stay away from berries and citrus fruits, which may release too much water as the cake bakes.

In the summer, my go-to fruit is cherries. Bing cherries have a long harvest season, but if you find Rainier, Bigarreau (my favorite), or sour cherries at the market, those work, too. In the winter, use brandied cherries like Luxardo maraschinos or Amarenas for an even richer cherry flavor; just be sure to drain them before adding them to the batter. As an alternative, bananas work well any time of year—try using Caramelized Bananas (page 238) for an extra layer of flavor.

THE CHANGE

Pit and quarter* **100 grams (1 cup) fresh Bing cherries**. In step 4 of **My Go-To Chocolate Cake** (page 22), whisk the wet ingredients into the dry ingredients as directed, then gently fold in the cherries until evenly distributed. Proceed as directed in the recipe, noting that the fruit in the batter means the cake may take just a few minutes longer to bake.

> * *Cutting fruit into small pieces—in this case, quarters—prevents it from sinking to the bottom of the cake. To further help suspend the cherries evenly throughout the cake, try tossing them in flour until very lightly coated before adding them to the batter.*

TWO IDEAS TO GET YOU STARTED

> One layer: Vanilla Chantilly Cream (page 252) and fresh cherries (page 248)

> Two layers: Cherry Jam (page 163) with Chocolate Buttercream (page 222)

SHOWSTOPPER

HAZELNUT CHOCOLATE CHERRY CAKE: Cherry Chocolate Cake (above) filled with Milk Chocolate Mousse (page 204, made with gianduja) and finished with Dark Chocolate Glaze (page 230)

ESPRESSO-SOAKED
CHOCOLATE CAKE

Here's another way to elevate chocolate cake: infuse it with an espresso syrup. Syrups add a subtle flavor to cake, but can also be used to make cake extra moist. You can make the syrup in advance—and even add a splash of coffee liqueur for a little something extra.

ESPRESSO ORANGE SYRUP

25 grams	2⅛ cups	water
125 grams	½ cup + 2 tablespoons	granulated sugar
85 grams	¼ cup (3 shots)	espresso
		zest of ½ orange, removed with a vegetable peeler
25 grams	2 ounces	coffee liqueur (optional)

EQUIPMENT
Pastry brush

THE CHANGE

1. Bake the cake: Bake **My Go-To Chocolate Cake** (page 22) as directed.

2. Meanwhile, make the espresso orange syrup: Combine the water, sugar, espresso, and orange zest in a small pot and bring to a boil over high heat, stirring until the sugar has dissolved. Strain the syrup; discard the orange zest. Let cool completely, then stir in the coffee liqueur (if using).

3. Unmold and soak the cake: Let the cake cool in the pan for 15 minutes before turning it out of the pan. While the cake is still warm,* poke some holes in it using a wooden skewer or fork. Brush the surface with a good amount of the espresso orange syrup—enough that it's nicely soaked through but not so much that it falls apart. The cake should feel wet to the touch, but shouldn't leak syrup. The soaked cake should be enjoyed the same day, so use or serve within 8 hours.

> * *A warm cake will absorb a lot more syrup. Alternatively, if you have chocolate cake stored, you can let it come to room temperature and then heat it up in the oven until warm (350°F [175°C] for 10 to 15 minutes).*

TWO IDEAS TO GET YOU STARTED

> One layer: Spiked Dark Chocolate Ganache (page 144, with Kahlúa)

> Two layers: Mascarpone Whipped Ganache (page 178) with Coffee Buttercream (page 222)

EXTRA SYRUPS FOR SOAKING THE CAKE

The secret to a moist cake may not be simply in the recipe, but in soaking the cake in syrup as well. It's a classic French technique that I've always loved because you can also lace your cake with the subtle flavor of the syrup.

MAKES: 500 grams or 2½ cups
TIME: 5 to 20 minutes

ROSE WATER SYRUP

250 grams	1¼ cups	granulated sugar
250 grams	1 cup	water
		A few drops rose water, to taste

Combine the sugar and water in a small saucepan and bring to a boil over medium heat, stirring occasionally to dissolve the sugar. Remove from the heat. Add the rose water and stir to combine. Let cool completely.

AMARETTO ESPRESSO SYRUP

420 grams	1¾ cups	brewed espresso, hot
80 grams	⅓ cup + 1 tablespoon	granulated sugar
20 grams	4½ teaspoons	amaretto*

Feel free to remove the alcohol if you want alcohol-free.

Stir together the espresso, sugar, and amaretto (if using) in a small bowl until the sugar has dissolved. Let cool completely.

ELDERFLOWER SYRUP

250 grams	1¼ cups	granulated sugar
250 grams	1 cup	water
250 grams	1 cup	St-Germain elderflower liqueur

Combine the sugar and water in a small saucepan and bring to a boil over medium heat, stirring occasionally to dissolve the sugar. Remove from the heat. Add the St-Germain and stir to combine. Let cool completely.

SWEET TEA SYRUP

420 grams	1¾ cups	water
2 grams	1 tablespoon	black tea leaves
80 grams	⅓ cup + 1 tablespoon	granulated sugar

In a small saucepan, bring the water to a boil over medium heat. Remove from the heat, add the tea leaves, and let stand for 4 minutes. Strain the tea through a fine-mesh sieve into a small heatproof bowl; discard the tea leaves. Add the sugar and stir until it has dissolved. Let cool completely.

MINT HONEY SYRUP

250 grams	1¼ cups	water
250 grams	¾ cup	honey
		Leaves from 2 sprigs fresh mint

Combine the water and honey in a small saucepan and bring to a boil over medium heat. Meanwhile, put the mint leaves on a cutting board and smash them with the back of a knife or spoon to release their oils. When the honey mixture comes to a boil, add the mint, reduce the heat to low, and simmer for 1 minute. Remove from the heat. Strain the syrup through a fine-mesh sieve into a small heatproof bowl; discard the mint. Let cool completely.

ORANGE BLOSSOM SYRUP

250 grams	1¼ cups	granulated sugar
250 grams	1 cup	water
		A few drops orange blossom extract, to taste

Combine the sugar and water in a small saucepan and bring to a boil over medium heat, stirring occasionally to dissolve the sugar. Remove from the heat. Add the orange blossom extract and stir to combine. Let cool completely.

RUM SYRUP

250 grams	1¼ cups	granulated sugar
250 grams	1 cup	water
20 grams	1½ tablespoons	rum

Combine the sugar and water in a small saucepan and bring to a boil over medium heat, stirring occasionally to dissolve the sugar. Remove from the heat and stir in the rum. Let cool completely.

BOURBON SYRUP

250 grams	1¼ cups	granulated sugar
250 grams	1 cup	water
20 grams	1½ tablespoons	bourbon

Combine the sugar and water in a small saucepan and bring to a boil over medium heat, stirring occasionally to dissolve the sugar. Remove from the heat and stir in the bourbon. Let cool completely.

STORAGE
The syrups can be stored in an airtight container in the refrigerator for up to 1 week.

MY GO-TO ALMOND CAKE

Maybe you wouldn't consider almond cake a staple, but over my years of working in the kitchen, it's become one of my go-tos. Plain sponge cakes are so often bland, but with the addition of almond flour, this recipe delivers so much more flavor—and is more moist. The result is light, but sturdy enough to build a layer cake.

MAKES: One 8-inch (20 cm) cake (about 2 to 2½ inches or 5 to 6.25 cm tall)
TIME: 50 minutes

INGREDIENTS

65 grams	1½ large	eggs
40 grams	2 large	egg yolks
75 grams	⅔ cup	confectioners' sugar
75 grams	¾ cup	almond flour
135 grams	4½ large	egg whites
50 grams	¼ cup	granulated sugar
60 grams	½ cup	all-purpose flour, sifted, plus more for the pan

EQUIPMENT
Stand mixer with whisk attachment

1. Preheat the oven: Preheat the oven to 350°F (175°C). Butter the bottom, sides, and edges of an 8-inch (20 cm) round cake pan. Pour in some flour and shake it around until the pan is evenly coated, then tap out any excess flour.

2. Make the egg yolk mixture: In a stand mixer fitted with the whisk attachment, combine the eggs, egg yolks, confectioners' sugar, and almond flour and whip on high speed until doubled in volume and light buttery yellow, 3 to 5 minutes. Transfer the egg yolk mixture to a large bowl.

3. Make the meringue: Wash and dry the mixer bowl and whisk attachment, then return both to the stand mixer. Put the egg whites in the mixer bowl and whip on medium-high speed until bubbles start to form, 2 to 3 minutes. With the mixer on low, slowly add the granulated sugar and mix until the meringue is shiny and holds medium-stiff peaks, 5 to 7 minutes.

4. Make the batter: Using a spatula, scoop one-quarter of the meringue into the egg yolk mixture and gently fold them together until fully combined (this lightens the denser egg yolk mixture so it doesn't deflate the rest of the meringue when you fold it in). Add the remaining meringue and gently fold until just combined (you should still be able to see a few streaks of meringue). Add the all-purpose flour and gently fold it in with a spatula until fully incorporated. Carefully, so as not to knock air out of the batter, pour the batter into the prepared pan.

5. Bake the cake: Bake the cake until lightly golden brown, about 25 minutes. There are three ways to check if it's done:

> *Jiggle it:* The cake should wiggle a little in the middle. If it wiggles a lot, it's not ready.

> *Nudge it:* Press the top gently; it should bounce back to your touch.

> *Poke it:* Stick a toothpick or paring knife into the center of the cake. If it comes out clean, it's done.

6. Unmold the cake: Let the cake cool in the pan for about 15 minutes. While the cake is still warm, place a large plate over it, then flip the plate and pan together; the cake should easily slide out of the pan onto the plate.

STORAGE

The cake is best enjoyed fresh the same day it's baked, but can be wrapped tightly with plastic wrap and refrigerated for up to 2 days. For longer storage, wrap it tightly with plastic wrap, place in an airtight container, and freeze for up to 3 weeks. To use a frozen cake, remove it from the airtight container and transfer it to the refrigerator to thaw for at least 3 hours or up to overnight, until the cake is soft again.

PAIR IT WITH

> **RECOMMENDED FILLINGS:** curd, jam, gelée, compote, ganache, mousse, whipped ganache

> **RECOMMENDED FINISHINGS:** buttercream, Italian meringue, glaze, Chantilly cream, streusel crumble, fruit

---

TWO IDEAS TO GET YOU STARTED

> One layer: Milk Chocolate Mousse (page 204)

> Two layers: Rhubarb Compote (page 153) with Toasted Hazelnut Meringue (page 265)

ROULADE

Since almond cake is moist and flexible, it is the perfect cake for making a roulade, or rolled cake. The only thing that's different from making a layer cake is that you would bake the batter in a sheet pan. To make a roulade:

1. Line a rimmed sheet pan with a silicone baking mat. Pour the batter into the pan and bake as directed on page 34, but check the cake sooner; it will likely bake faster, 15 minutes or less.

2. Let the cake cool in the pan for a few minutes. When it is cool enough to handle but still warm, flip the pan over a cutting board and pull off the silicone mat. Let cool completely. Soak with a syrup to keep the cake moist (I like an Elderflower Syrup—page 30).

3. Spread a ⅛-inch-thick layer of cream (I like Chantilly cream or Vanilla Whipped Ganache, page 187) over the entire surface of the cake. You can also add jam or even small diced fresh fruit.

4. Starting from one long side, slowly roll up the cake into a log. Clean off any cream escaping from the ends. Wrap the log tightly in plastic wrap and refrigerate for 2 hours (this helps the cake hold its shape).

5. Unwrap the cake, transfer it to a serving plate, and finish with a dusting of confectioners' sugar or more cream and fruit. Once assembled, the roulade can be kept refrigerated for up to 2 days.

APRICOT ELDERFLOWER ROULADE

BASE: Almond Cake (page 34) + Elderflower Syrup (page 30)

FILLING: Vanilla Whipped Ganache (page 187) + Apricot Gelée (page 168)

FINISHING: Fresh apricots (page 248) + Nappage Glaze (page 223)

TECHNIQUE: Roulade (page 36)

MATCHA ALMOND CAKE

BASE

MY GO-TO ALMOND CAKE

Matcha powder gives this variation of My Go-To Almond Cake a fragrant green tea flavor—it's also slightly less sweet.

THE CHANGE

In step 4 of **My Go-To Almond Cake** (page 34), after folding together the egg yolk mixture and the meringue, add **7 grams (1 tablespoon) matcha green tea powder**, then the all-purpose flour. Gently fold it in with a spatula until fully incorporated. Proceed with the recipe as directed.

TWO IDEAS TO GET YOU STARTED

> One layer: White Chocolate Glaze (page 234)

> Two layers: Coconut Whipped Ganache (page 181), between the layers and on top

MOLASSES ALMOND CAKE

Adding molasses gives an otherwise mild-flavored almond cake surprising richness.

THE CHANGE

In step 2 of **My Go-To Almond Cake** (page 34), add **50 grams (2½ tablespoons) molasses*** with the eggs, egg yolks, confectioners' sugar, and almond flour. Proceed with the recipe as directed. Because of the addition of the molasses, this cake will be darker, and it may be more difficult to tell if it's ready to come out of the oven.

> * *To make life a little easier, when measuring sticky ingredients—molasses, maple syrup, honey, and more—first lightly coat the measuring spoon with nonstick cooking spray or a little bit of neutral oil (like vegetable oil or canola oil), then measure the ingredient. It will slide right out of the measuring spoon into your bowl . . . meaning less mess and a more accurate measurement.*

TWO IDEAS TO GET YOU STARTED

> One layer: Cream Cheese Buttercream (page 222)

> Two layers: Apple Compote (page 150) with Chestnut-Whiskey Chantilly Cream (page 253)

SHOWSTOPPER

FIG MOLASSES OLIVE OIL CAKE (page 197): Molasses Almond Cake filled with Olive Oil Mousse (page 196) and Fig Jam (page 162) and finished with fresh figs (page 248) and Vanilla Chantilly Cream (page 252)

OLIVE OIL ALMOND CAKE

MY GO-TO ALMOND CAKE

One of my favorite ways to vary pound cake and almond cake is to add olive oil. It not only adds moisture, giving the cake an even more decadent texture, but also lends flavor and fragrance. I use a good-quality green olive oil, one that tastes bold and grassy, for the most delicious cake and a hint of green color.

THE CHANGE

In step 4 of **My Go-To Almond Cake** (page 34), after folding together the egg yolk mixture and the meringue, gently fold in **60 grams (4 tablespoons) high-quality extra-virgin olive oil*** 1 tablespoon at a time, alternating with the all-purpose flour. Proceed with the recipe as directed.

> * *This cake will be buttery yellow when baked. When I want a light green olive oil cake, I drizzle in a few drops of pumpkin seed oil along with the olive oil until I get the right color of green.*

TWO IDEAS TO GET YOU STARTED

> One layer: Roasted Figs (page 246) spooned on the side
> Two layers: Lemon Curd (page 134) and Tarragon Chantilly Cream (page 253)

It's Just Like Kindergarten: Start with the Fundamentals

On my first day of kindergarten, I learned the alphabet. I remember how at first the letters were just symbols with no meaning, hieroglyphics I couldn't yet decipher. Then the teacher walked us through each one and taught us that they represented a sound. And the singing began. In France, just like in the United States, the alphabet is always sung to the same familiar tune. I sang along, sounding out the letters one by one, not knowing then that these letters would become words, and the words would become sentences, and the sentences would become chapters and stories and books.

At the end of that day, my teacher pulled my mom aside. She told my mom that I was different than the other kids. All day, I sang the alphabet song over and over again. While the other kids giggled and sometimes would lose interest and do something else, I tried singing the alphabet song faster, then slower, then backward. I was obsessed with getting it right.

On my first day of culinary school, thirteen years later, I learned the chef's equivalent of the alphabet. We set up our station, or *mise en place*, as we call it in French. There was a cutting board in the center and small stainless-steel bowls on one side to be filled by a mishmosh of ingredients: salt, pepper, sugar, and spices ranging from cayenne to herbes de Provence to saffron. And on the other side was our sharpened knife, ready to begin its work. To my surprise, we did not cook at all—that would come later. Instead, we cut, chopped, peeled, sliced, and then washed. Dressed in starch-stiff chef whites and paper chef toques, with our backs straight, the other students and I followed each step carefully. I looked at my station in front of me—just a small space, about shoulder width, on a stainless-steel countertop—and learned my first lesson as a cook. The day passed, the Band-Aids came out. Students who lost focus cut themselves. Some became frustrated as we struggled to complete each step with the speed or precision the instructor required. This, I realized, was the stress of life in the kitchen. And it was then that the alphabet song strangely came into my head.

I started to hum it under my breath, and almost instantly, I felt the pressure of the instructor's demands lift. It's no wonder—the alphabet song shares the same calming melody as "Twinkle, Twinkle, Little Star." How curious, I thought, that the first song we learned in

school sounds like the lullaby that sent many of us to sleep when we were babies. As the song repeated in my head, I practiced each step of the mise en place over and over again.

Think of each recipe like a first day of school, and remember this as you read and bake. The first day of school has no tests, no homework, no deadlines. Instead, it introduces the fundamentals: your alphabet, your mise en place. As hard as it may seem when you first try, it'll be second nature to you in time if you repeat it carefully and often.

Focus. Relax. Learn to love the basics. The first few lessons in any curriculum are the ones you never forget. They are indispensable, because they open up limitless possibilities. The alphabet becomes great novels; the mise en place turns into fine dining. And recipes and cookbooks become the backbone to your own creations.

Back in kindergarten, it took a full two weeks before I stopped annoying my family with the alphabet song. But when the teacher asked who had memorized the alphabet, my hand shot up. I remember reciting the whole song in front of the class. When I neared that final letter, "Z," I smiled. *"Maintenant je connais mon alphabet,"* I sang. Next step: everything else.

MY GO-TO LADYFINGERS

This recipe is extremely versatile: once piped into your desired shape, it can be rolled around a filling, stacked and soaked, or wrapped around a cake. One common use of ladyfingers is to make the classic Tiramisu (page 53), but I also love to use it for the traditional French Charlotte, a cake that has a "fence" of ladyfingers surrounding a mousse center (page 56). On their own ladyfingers were made for dipping into coffee, tea, or—during the holidays—a glass of Champagne.

MAKES: One 8-inch (20 cm) round cake or 20 to 25 (4-inch or 10 cm) ladyfingers
TIME: 15 to 20 minutes for ladyfingers

INGREDIENTS

85 grams	4 large	egg yolks
130 grams	⅔ cup	granulated sugar
130 grams	4 large	egg whites
135 grams	1 cup	all-purpose flour, plus more for the pan
22 grams	7 teaspoons	cornstarch
38 grams	3 tablespoons	confectioners' sugar

EQUIPMENT

Stand mixer with whisk attachment (I don't recommend making this recipe by hand)

8-inch (20 cm) round cake pan (for cake)

Permanent marker and ruler (for ladyfingers)

Piping bag and large round piping tip (at least ½ inch or 1.5 cm opening; for ladyfingers)

1. Preheat the oven: Preheat the oven to 400°F (205°C). Line a sheet pan with parchment paper and use a permanent marker and a ruler to draw lines roughly 4 inches (10 cm) apart on the parchment; this will be your reference for how long each ladyfinger should be. Flip the parchment stencil ink-side down on the sheet pan.

2. Make the egg yolk mixture: In a stand mixer fitted with the whisk attachment, combine the egg yolks and 65 grams (½ cup) of the granulated sugar and whip on high speed until the mixture increases in volume and turns pale, 3 to 5 minutes. Pour into a large bowl.

3. Whip the egg whites: Wash and dry the mixer bowl and whisk attachment, then return both to the stand mixer. Put the egg whites in the mixer bowl and whip on high speed until they hold stiff peaks.* With the mixer on high speed, slowly add the remaining 65 grams (⅓ cup) granulated sugar and whip until fully incorporated.

> * *While you're whipping the egg whites, stop the mixer periodically and lift the whisk out of the bowl; if the egg whites stand upright without wilting or falling, that's stiff peaks.*

4. Make the batter: Gently fold the yolk mixture into the egg white mixture with a spatula until just incorporated. Be careful not to overmix as it will deflate the batter. Add the flour and cornstarch and gently fold until they are fully incorporated.

5. Scoop the batter into a piping bag fitted with a large round piping tip.* Pipe 4-inch-long (10 cm) ladyfingers onto the prepared sheet pan, using the marker line as a guide and spacing them at least 1 inch (2.5 cm) apart. Using a fine-mesh sieve, sprinkle the ladyfingers evenly with 1½ tablespoons of the confectioners' sugar.* Let sit for 5 minutes, then sprinkle evenly with another 1½ tablespoons confectioners' sugar.

> * *To easily fill your piping bag, put the bag in a quart container and fold the top of the bag over the rim of the container to hold it open while you pour in the batter.*

> * *Sprinkling the batter with confectioners' sugar gives the ladyfingers extra-crackly tops when baked.*

6. Bake the ladyfingers: Bake until the top of the ladyfingers are golden blond and the center is cooked through (it'll still be a bit moist), about 15 minutes. Press the top gently; it should bounce back to your touch.

7. Unmold the ladyfingers: Let the ladyfingers cool completely in the pan. Gently remove them from the parchment once cool.

STORAGE

The ladyfingers can be wrapped tightly with plastic wrap and stored on the counter or in the refrigerator for up to 2 days. For longer storage, wrap tightly with plastic wrap, place in an airtight container, and freeze for up to 3 weeks. To use frozen ladyfingers, remove from the airtight container and transfer to the refrigerator (still in the plastic wrap) to thaw for at least 3 hours or up to overnight, until soft again.

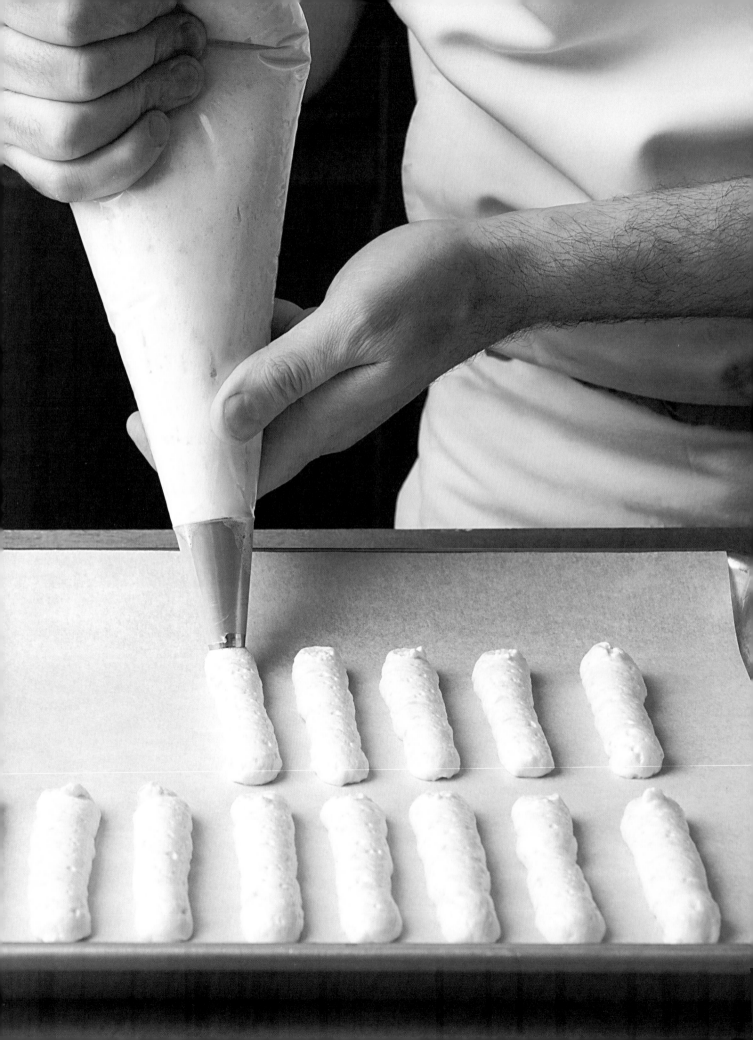

PAIR IT WITH

> **RECOMMENDED FILLINGS:** pastry cream, mousse, jam, whipped ganache

> **RECOMMENDED FINISHINGS:** Chantilly cream, Italian meringue, fruit

TWO IDEAS TO GET YOU STARTED

> Hazelnut Pastry Cream (page 121) and Italian Meringue (page 258)

> Pear Mousse (page 193) and Caramelized Pears (page 241)

CITRUS ALMOND CAKE OR LADYFINGERS

**MY GO-TO
LADYFINGERS**

Add citrus zest to almond cake or ladyfingers for a refreshing zing. For this recipe, you can use any citrus fruit—lemons (I like using Meyer lemons, which are a little less tangy), orange, lime, and grapefruit all work well.

THE CHANGE

In step 5 of **My Go-To Almond Cake** (page 34), after dusting the batter for the cake or ladyfingers with confectioners' sugar, sprinkle **the zest from one lemon (about 1 tablespoon or 6 grams**, or the same measurement of orange, lime, or grapefruit zest) over the sugar. Proceed with the recipe as directed.

TWO IDEAS TO GET YOU STARTED

> For a Lime Almond Cake: Blackberry Pastry Cream (page 121) with Greek Yogurt Chantilly Cream (page 253)

> For an Orange Almond Cake: Olive Oil Mousse (page 196) with Chocolate Meringue (page 260)

SOAKED LADYFINGERS

Another way to add flavor to ladyfingers is with a syrup. Here are two very different syrups—one delicate, one bold—to brush onto ladyfingers after they've baked.

ROSE WATER SYRUP (PAGE 29)

ESPRESSO SYRUP

| 420 grams | ¾ cup | brewed espresso, hot |
| 150 grams | ¾ cup | granulated sugar |

ADDED EQUIPMENT
Pastry brush

THE CHANGE

Prepare the ladyfingers as directed and let cool completely, then brush the surface with the rose water syrup or espresso syrup. Don't completely soak the ladyfingers; they should be moist but not so wet that they're falling apart. The soaked ladyfingers should be enjoyed the same day, so use or serve within 1–2 hours.

STORAGE

You will only use a few teaspoons of the syrup, so you'll have quite a bit left over. I like to use mine to flavor tea. The syrups will keep in the refrigerater for at least 2 weeks.

See additional syrups for soaking on page 29.

TIRAMISU

Tiramisu is one of the desserts I order most frequently at restaurants. There's something about that perfect match of textures and flavors that make this an undeniable classic. And even though I order this dessert at restaurants, tiramisus are easy to build and make at home, once you have all your ingredients together.

1. Brush or dip baked piped ladyfingers generously in Amaretto Espresso Syrup (page 29).

2. Line the bottom of a glass baking tray with a layer of soaked ladyfingers. If needed, break some in half to cover the entire surface area.

3. Top with a layer of Mascarpone Whipped Ganache (page 178), roughly 1.5 inches thick.

4. Repeat with another layer of soaked ladyfingers and another layer of whipped ganache.

5. Finish with a generous dusting of unsweetened cocoa powder.

For a different take on the traditional tiramisu, brush the ladyfingers with Rose Water Syrup (page 29) and fill with Pistachio Chantilly Cream (page 253), and top with chopped pistachios. Once assembled, the tiramisu can be kept refrigerated for up to 4 days.

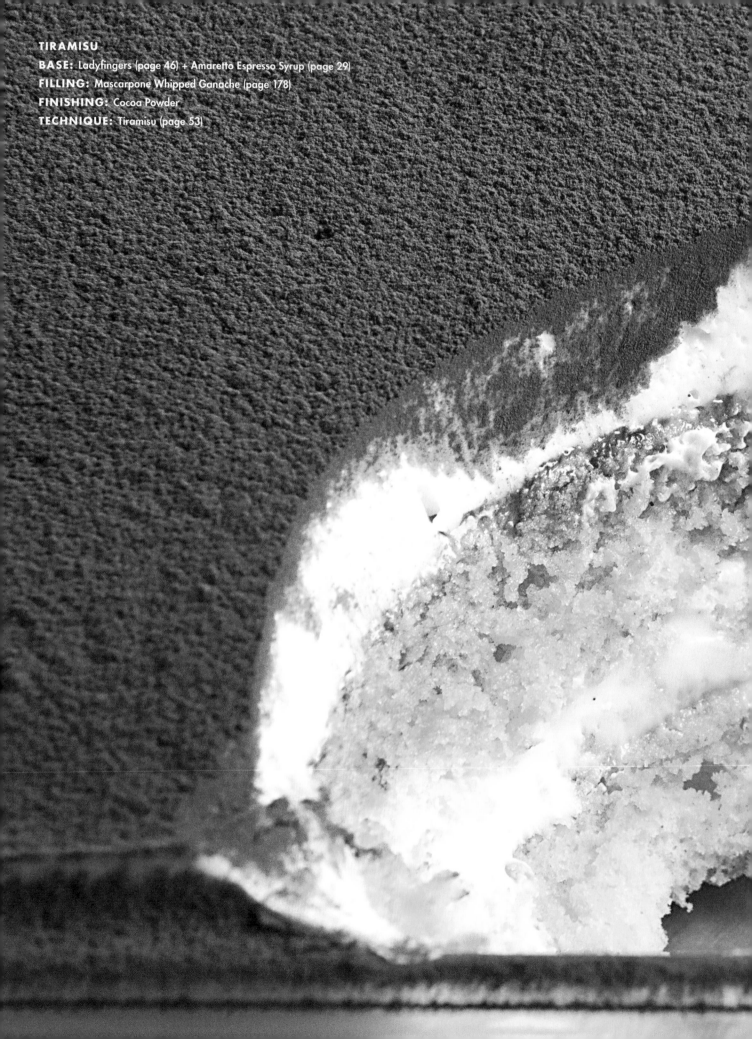

TIRAMISU
BASE: Ladyfingers (page 46) + Amaretto Espresso Syrup (page 29)
FILLING: Mascarpone Whipped Ganache (page 178)
FINISHING: Cocoa Powder
TECHNIQUE: Tiramisu (page 53)

CHARLOTTE

You may not be familiar with a Charlotte, but it is a classic dessert found in many pastry shops in France. Essentially it is a pastry base surrounded by a ring of ladyfingers, arranged vertically, almost like a crown. The cake can be filled with mousses, whipped ganaches or creams, and fresh fruit. The main difference between a Charlotte and a Tiramisu is that in addition to the ladyfingers, you also pipe a base—using the same batter.

1. Pipe a batch of ladyfingers according to the directions on page 46. Make a second batch of batter. Use an 8-inch (20 cm) ring as a guide, and trace a circle on a piece of parchment paper. Flip the parchment over, and pipe the base to fill the stencil.

2. Bake the ladyfingers and the base according to the directions on page 46.

3. Using a pastry brush, soak the base and the ladyfingers with syrup (I love the Rose Water Syrup, page 29). Place the base on the bottom of the cake ring. Line the inside of the cake ring with ladyfingers, arranged vertically, with no space in between.

4. Spread a thick layer of jam onto the base (Try Strawberry Jam, page 159).

5. Fill the rest of the Charlotte with a whipped ganache (I like Muscovado Sugar Whipped Ganache, page 186) and top with fresh fruits, such as peaches or berries (page 248).

6. Finish using a pastry brush—lightly brush a thin layer of Nappage Glaze (page 223) to cover the Charlotte completely. Once assembled, the Charlotte can be kept refrigerated for up to 2 days.

PEACH BROWN SUGAR CHARLOTTE

BASE: Ladyfingers (page 46) + Rose Water Syrup (page 29)

FILLING: Strawberry Jam (page 159) + Muscovado Sugar Whipped Ganache (page 186) + Fresh peaches (page 248)

FINISHING: Nappage Glaze (page 223)

TECHNIQUE: Charlotte (page 56)

MY GO-TO BANANA BREAD

I tasted banana bread for the first time when I moved to America. Even though it's traditionally baked in a loaf pan, I loved its flavor so much that I thought it could be a component to build even more desserts. Its forgiving texture—moist and easy to slice—allowed me to experiment with it. I built it into layer cakes. I added ingredients—like pumpkin, strawberry, and zucchini, and I loved those variations, too. Think about that classic banana bread differently, and try elevating it to new levels.

MAKES: One 8-inch (20 cm) round cake or one 8½ x 4½-inch (21 x 11 cm) loaf cake
TIME: About 1 hour 30 minutes

INGREDIENTS

400 grams	2 cups	granulated sugar
250 grams	2 cups	all-purpose flour, plus more for dusting
3 grams	¾ teaspoon	baking soda
2 grams	¾ teaspoon	ground nutmeg
5 grams	1 teaspoon	salt
5 grams	1 teaspoon	baking powder
150 grams	3 large	eggs
400 grams	2 cups (about 4)	overripe bananas, peeled and mashed
200 grams	14 tablespoons (1¾ sticks)	unsalted butter, melted, plus more for greasing

EQUIPMENT
8-inch (20 cm) round cake pan or 8½ x 4½-inch (21 x 11 cm) loaf pan

1. Preheat the oven: Preheat the oven to 350°F (175°C). Butter the bottom, sides, and edges of an 8-inch (20 cm) round cake pan or 8½ x 4½-inch (21 x 11 cm) loaf pan. Pour in some flour and shake it around until the pan is evenly coated, then tap out any excess flour.*

> * If you're using a loaf pan, you can line the bottom and sides with parchment paper instead of buttering and flouring it. (This makes cleanup a little easier.)

2. Combine the dry ingredients: Combine the sugar, flour, baking soda, nutmeg, salt, and baking powder in a large bowl.

3. Make the batter: Whisk the eggs in a separate large bowl. Mix in the mashed bananas. Pour the egg mixture over the dry ingredients and whisk until well combined. Stir in the melted butter.

4. Bake the cake: Pour the batter into the prepared pan, filling it to ¾ inch (2 cm) from the top (you may have extra batter). Bake until the cake is golden brown, about 1 hour. There are three ways to check if it's done:

> *Jiggle it:* The cake should wiggle a little in the middle. If it wiggles a lot, it's not ready.
> *Nudge it:* Press the top gently; it should bounce back to your touch.
> *Poke it:* Stick a toothpick or paring knife into the center of the cake. If it comes out clean, it's done.

5. Cool and unmold the cake: Let the cake cool in the pan for 15 minutes. While the cake is still warm, turn it out of the pan. Let cool completely if using it to build a layer cake. Otherwise, slice and eat while still warm.

STORAGE

The banana bread can be wrapped tightly in plastic wrap or placed in an airtight container and stored at room temperature for up to 2 days. For longer storage, wrap it tightly in plastic wrap, place in an airtight container, and freeze for up to 3 weeks. To use the frozen banana bread, remove it from the airtight container and transfer it to the refrigerator (still in the plastic wrap) to thaw for at least 3 hours or up to overnight, until the banana bread is soft again.

PAIR IT WITH

> **RECOMMENDED FILLINGS:** curd, jam, compote, mousse, whipped ganache
> **RECOMMENDED FINISHINGS:** buttercream, glaze, streusel crumble

TWO IDEAS TO GET YOU STARTED

> One layer: Slice, toast, and slather with butter and jam
> Two layers: Peanut Butter Mousse (page 195), between the layers and on top, with Caramelized Bananas (page 238)

SHOWSTOPPER

BANANA BREAD (page 58): Finished with Caramelized Bananas (page 238) and Chestnut-Whiskey Chantilly Cream (page 253)

STRAWBERRY BANANA BREAD

MY GO-TO BANANA BREAD

To give My Go-To Banana Bread an extra burst of flavor, I like to incorporate more fruit—in this case, dried strawberries—into the batter. Use dried fruits here; fresh fruits will release water as they bake, and you'll be left with soggy banana bread.

THE CHANGE

Prepare the batter for **My Go-To Banana Bread** (page 60) as directed, then fold in **90 grams (½ cup) dried strawberries**, coarsely chopped.* Proceed with the recipe as directed.

> * *Chopping strawberries into smaller pieces prevents them from sinking straight to the bottom of the batter.*

TWO IDEAS TO GET YOU STARTED

> One layer: Slice, toast, and slather with butter and strawberry jam
> Two layers: Muscovado Sugar Whipped Ganache (page 186), between the layers and on top, with fresh strawberries (page 248)

PUMPKIN BANANA BREAD

BASE

MY GO-TO BANANA BREAD

When summer turns to autumn, I love to bake with pumpkin. This variation of My Go-To Banana Bread incorporates pumpkin purée which makes the texture even more moist and gives it a light orange color.

THE CHANGE

In step 3 of **My Go-To Banana Bread** (page 60), reduce the quantity of bananas to 300 grams (1½ cups; about 3 bananas, peeled and mashed) and add **200 grams (1½ cups) pumpkin purée** with the mashed bananas. Proceed with the recipe as directed. The pumpkin will add a little more moisture to the batter, so you may need to bake the bread for just a few seconds longer. The top may also crack a bit more than the Go-To Banana Bread, but you can trim it or cover it with any number of fillings or finishings.

TWO IDEAS TO GET YOU STARTED

> One layer: Slice, toast, and slather with butter
> Two layers: Olive Oil Mousse (page 196) with Caramel Glaze (page 227)

ZUCCHINI BANANA BREAD

MY GO-TO BANANA BREAD

Zucchini may seem a strange ingredient to add to desserts, but once shredded, it becomes a "moisture booster," a perfect addition for a tender and moist cake. Handle the zucchini carefully and add it at the end of the recipe to not break it up too much. After it's baked, the zucchini breaks down and almost disappears, leaving little of its taste.

THE CHANGE

In step 3 of **My Go-To Banana Bread** (page 60), reduce the quantity of bananas to 200 grams (1 cup; about 2 bananas) and add **200 grams (2 cups) shredded zucchini*** with the mashed bananas. Proceed with the recipe as directed*.

* *You do not need to peel the zucchini—the skin is tender and delicious!*

* *With the addition of zucchini, there's a little more moisture in the batter: you may need to bake the cake for just a few seconds longer.*

TWO IDEAS TO GET YOU STARTED

> One layer: Slice, toast, and slather with butter
> Two layers: Lemon Curd (page 134) with Cream Cheese Buttercream (page 222)

One Cake Recipe Can Lead to Unlimited Possibilities

Mention *gâteau au yaourt* to anyone French, and they'll likely smile and begin to reminisce. Every kid I knew growing up made this dessert at one time or another. The recipe was easy to commit to memory . . . and it never failed. It began with a container of yogurt, on which was written a recipe: empty the container of yogurt into a mixing bowl, then use the empty container to measure out two servings of sugar, three servings of flour, half a serving of oil, and three eggs. A pinch of salt and a splash of vanilla and there you have it—the first cake I ever made. Every batch resulted in the same light, moist pound cake, which I would carefully ration throughout the week as an after-school snack.

At a certain point, I grew tired of the yogurt cake's subtle flavor. I started adding nuts, chocolate, or lemon zest to create new tastes and textures. The base cake batter became a canvas. I'm still amazed by the resilience of the recipe, and how it could withstand the culinary machinations of a kid and still deliver a reliably delicious result.

You know that saying "Everything I need to know, I learned in kindergarten"? Well, I learned much of what I know about recipe development from that the basic yogurt cake, which I first attempted in elementary school. The first lesson begins with the yogurt container. Using the same vessel to measure my flour, oil, and sugar meant I had a standardized measuring tool. I can't tell you the number of times I've emphasized this to professional cooks and home cooks alike: precise measurements are the key to acing a recipe. Measuring eggs by weight is certainly better than cracking a certain number of eggs into your mixture, as the size of each egg varies. Buy a scale. It is a tool that sets you up for success.

The second lesson comes from the ingredients. I used the same trusted brand of yogurt every time I baked a yogurt cake. Over time, I discovered that the larger the batch, small variations in quality can alter the results. In our kitchens today, which produce hundreds of cakes, even the season when the grains for your flour were harvested can lead to something unexpected. Macarons made from almonds in the summertime can sometimes be oilier due to the fattiness of the summer harvest. A croissant made from a lower-quality butter will be chewier and doughier rather than flaky and light.

The third and last lesson—and perhaps the most important—comes from those culinary machinations. I mastered a basic recipe and then I began to change it slightly. I didn't change the measurements, key ingredients, or proportions—those should be meticulously followed. But once you have perfected a recipe, you can experiment. I added nuts, chocolate, or lemon zest to stretch and twist the recipe in new directions. When you have your groundwork laid out, the future is full of possibilities. All the go-to recipes in this book offer you that starting point. Learn them well, and then begin to add your special touches.

A few years ago in New York, far away from my hometown in France, a friend of mine surprised me with a yogurt cake. It was made using a very similar recipe to the one from my childhood: the familiar loaf shape with soft rounded edges, the golden dome top complete with a center crack, and the spongy interior that looks almost perforated with microbubbles. I took a bite. "How does it taste?" he asked. "Similar, but different," I answered. "Which is a good thing."

LEMON POUND CAKE
BASE: Lemon Pound Cake (page 72)
FINISHING: Nappage Glaze (page 223)

MY GO-TO
VANILLA POUND CAKE

Pound cakes are sturdy: they travel well and keep well. If you need a cake to bring to someone's home, this would be my suggestion. I like to eat my pound cake plain—a thick slice goes well with a cup of tea.

MAKES: One 8-inch (20 cm) round cake (2 to 2½ inches or 5 to 6.25 cm tall) or one 8½ x 4½-inch (21 x 11 cm) loaf cake
TIME: 1 hour 30 minutes

INGREDIENTS

225 grams	4 large	eggs
265 grams	1⅓ cups	granulated sugar
135 grams	½ cup	crème fraîche, at room temperature
240 grams	2 cups	all-purpose flour, plus more for dusting
4 grams	¾ teaspoon	baking powder
2 grams	⅓ teaspoon	salt
90 grams	6 tablespoons (¾ stick)	unsalted butter
6 grams	1	Tahition vanilla bean, split lengthwise, seeds scraped

EQUIPMENT

8-inch (20 cm) round cake pan or 8½ x 4½-inch (21 x 11 cm) loaf pan
Stand mixer with whisk attachment or hand mixer

1. Preheat the oven: Preheat the oven to 325°F (160°C). Butter the bottom, sides, and edges of an 8-inch (20 cm) cake pan or 8½ x 4½-inch (21 x 11 cm) loaf pan.* Pour in some flour and shake it around until the pan is evenly coated, then tap out any excess flour.

> * If you're using a loaf pan, you can line the bottom and sides with parchment paper instead of buttering and flouring it. (This makes cleanup a little easier.)

2. Make the egg mixture: In a stand mixer fitted with the whisk attachment (or in a large bowl using a hand mixer), combine the eggs and sugar and whip on high speed until smooth and lightened in color, 2 to 3 minutes. Put the crème fraîche in a medium bowl, add a large scoop of the egg mixture, and whisk it into the crème fraîche to lighten it. Add the crème fraîche to the bowl with the remaining egg mixture and gently whisk until fully incorporated.

3. Combine the dry ingredients: Whisk together the flour, baking powder, and salt in a separate medium bowl to break up any lumps.

4. Make the batter: Fold the dry ingredients into the egg mixture in thirds, folding until combined after each addition.

5. Combine the butter and vanilla seeds in a small heatproof bowl. Microwave* in 30-second increments, stirring after each to prevent burning, until the butter has melted. While whisking, slowly pour the melted butter into the batter and whisk until combined.

> * *If you prefer not to use a microwave, melt the butter in a small pot over low heat. Remove it from the heat as soon as the butter has melted—you don't want the butter to brown.*

6. If you're using a cake pan, **pour the batter into the prepared pan** until it reaches halfway up the sides; if you're using a loaf pan, fill it to about ½ inch (1.5 cm) from the top.

7. Bake the cake: Bake until the cake is golden brown, 55 minutes to 1 hour.

8. Unmold the cake: Let the cake cool in the pan for 15 minutes. While the cake is still warm, turn it out of the pan, then turn it right side up, and let cool completely.

STORAGE

The pound cake is best enjoyed the same day it's baked, but can be wrapped tightly in plastic wrap or placed in an airtight container and stored at room temperature for up to 2 days. For longer storage, wrap it tightly in plastic wrap, place in an airtight container, and freeze for up to 3 weeks. To use the frozen loaf, remove it from the airtight container and transfer it to the refrigerator (still in the plastic wrap) to thaw for at least 3 hours or overnight, until the loaf cake is soft again.

PAIR IT WITH

> **RECOMMENDED FILLINGS:** curd, jam, gelée, compote, ganache, mousse, whipped ganache

> **RECOMMENDED FINISHINGS:** buttercream, Italian meringue, glaze, Chantilly cream, streusel crumble, fruit

---

TWO IDEAS TO GET YOU STARTED

> One layer: Earl Grey Italian Meringue (page 261)

> Two layers: Crème Fraîche Whipped Ganache (page 184), between layers and on top, with sliced fresh peaches (page 248)

LEMON POUND CAKE

MY GO-TO VANILLA POUND CAKE

Adding fresh lemon juice and lemon zest to My Go-To Vanilla Pound Cake gives the classic a bright, citrusy kick. You can use regular lemons for this recipe, or try Meyer lemons for a milder, more floral citrus aroma.

THE CHANGE

In step 4 of **My Go-To Vanilla Pound Cake** (page 70), whisk **12 grams (2 teaspoons) lemon zest (from 1 lemon)** into the dry ingredients. Make the batter as directed, but in step 5, replace the vanilla seeds with **100 grams (½ cup) fresh lemon juice**. Proceed with the recipe as directed.

TWO IDEAS TO GET YOU STARTED

> One layer: Lavender Dark Chocolate Ganache (page 142)
> Two layers: Lemon Curd (page 134) with Raspberry Meringue (page 264)

SHOWSTOPPER

LEMON POUND CAKE WITH NAPPAGE GLAZE (page 223)

GINGER POUND CAKE

**MY GO-TO VANILLA
POUND CAKE**

I love the flavor of fresh ginger, and it works well with rich, buttery flavors like those in My Go-To Vanilla Pound Cake, giving it a subtle hint of warm spice. Using fresh ginger rather than ground ginger means you'll get a more potent kick; ground ginger tends to be subtler.

THE CHANGE

In step 5 of **My Go-To Vanilla Pound Cake** (page 70), replace the vanilla seeds with **12 grams (2 tablespoons) grated fresh ginger**. Proceed with the recipe as directed.

TWO IDEAS TO GET YOU STARTED

> One layer: Dark Chocolate Mousse (page 200) and Caramelized Pears (page 244)

> Two layers: Coconut Whipped Ganache (page 181) with Cream Cheese Buttercream (page 222)

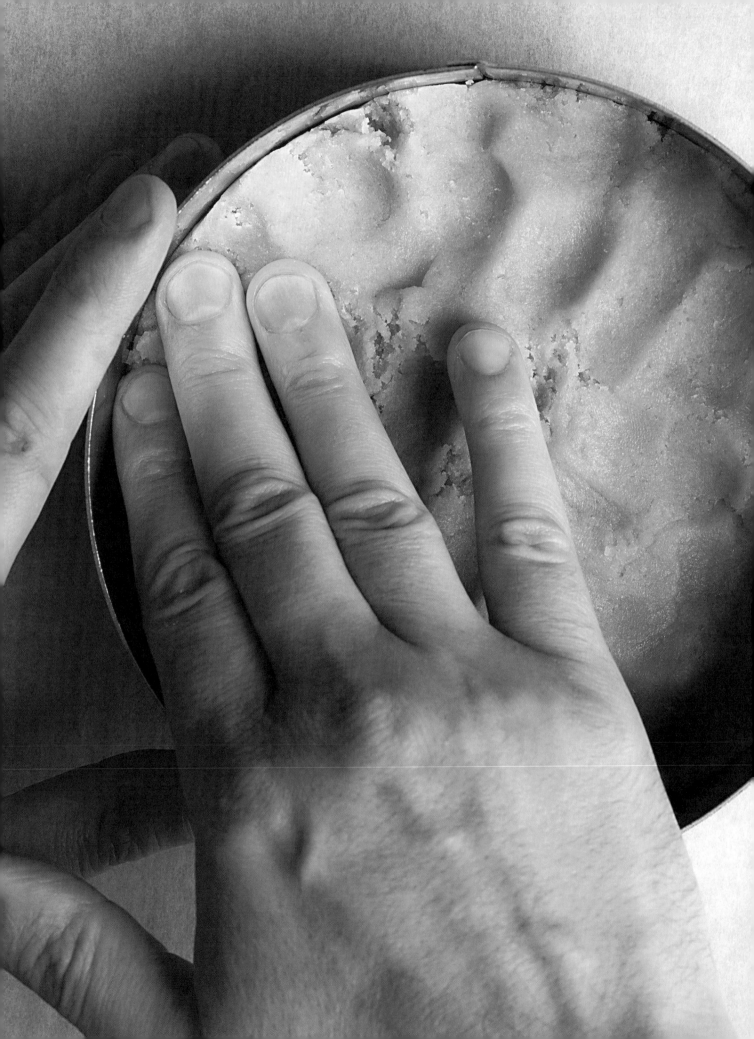

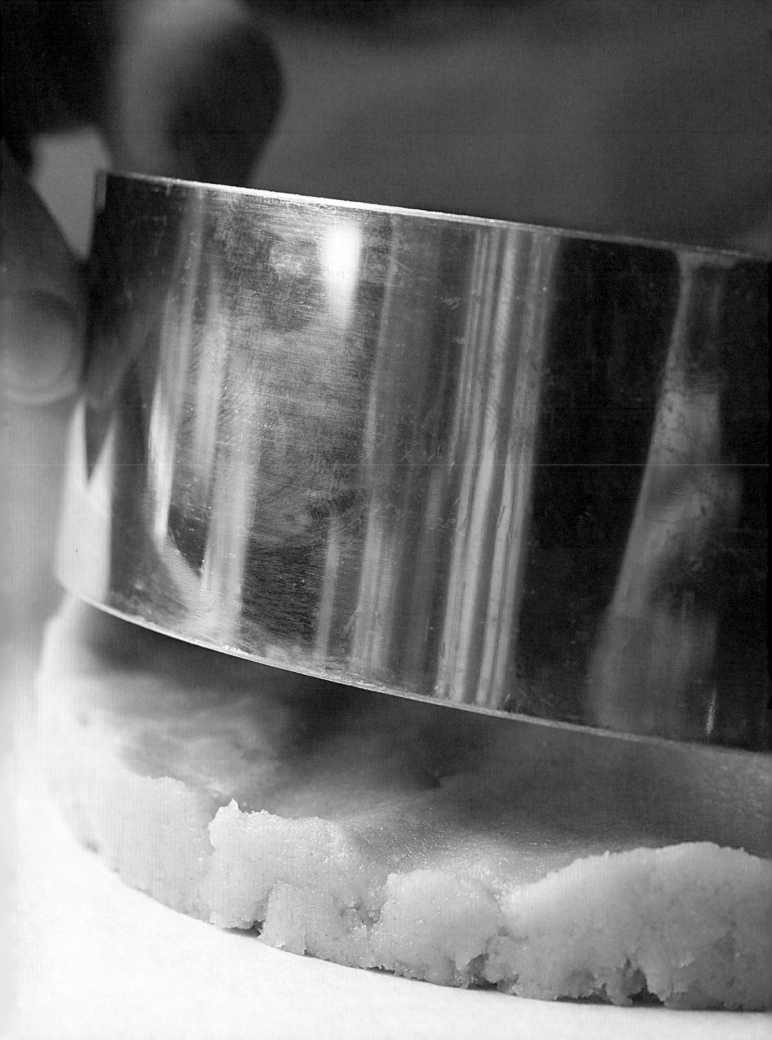

MY GO-TO COOKIE BASE

Soft and chewy, this cookie base can make a delicious—and surprising!—addition to a mousse cake. And if you don't have the patience to build a cake, portion this dough for individual cookies, bake, and enjoy with a cold glass of milk.

MAKES: One 8-inch (20 cm) cookie base or 6 to 8 large cookies
TIME: 50 minutes

INGREDIENTS

95 grams	7 tablespoons	unsalted butter, cut into cubes, at room temperature
65 grams	⅓ cup	granulated sugar
65 grams	⅓ cup	packed light brown sugar
40 grams	1 large	egg
165 grams	1⅓ cups	all-purpose flour, plus more for dusting
2 grams	½ teaspoon	baking soda
3 grams	½ teaspoon	salt

EQUIPMENT

Stand mixer with paddle attachment or hand mixer
8-inch (20 cm) round cake ring (optional, for cookie base)

1. **Preheat the oven:** Preheat the oven to 350°F (175°C). Line a sheet pan with parchment paper.

2. **Combine the wet ingredients:** In a stand mixer fitted with the paddle attachment (or in a large bowl using a hand mixer), combine the butter, granulated sugar, and brown sugar and beat on medium-high speed until light and fluffy, 2 to 3 minutes. Add the egg and beat until incorporated.

3. **Combine the dry ingredients:** Whisk together the flour, baking soda, and salt in a medium bowl.

4. **Make the dough:** With the mixer on low, slowly add the dry ingredients to the wet ingredients. Mix until just combined. (At this point, the dough can be refrigerated for later use—see Storage.)

5. **Shape the dough:** Dust your work surface with flour. For a cake base, dust an 8-inch (20 cm) round cake ring with flour. Roll out the dough to ½ inch (1.5 cm) thick, then use the floured cake ring to punch out a disc of dough. Transfer the disc of dough, still in the

cake ring, to the prepared sheet pan. For individual cookies, roll the dough into balls about 2 inches (5 cm) in diameter, place them on the prepared sheet pan, and press down slightly to flatten them into discs.

6. Bake the cookie(s): If you are baking a cookie base (think of it as one large cookie), it takes longer—bake for 17 to 20 minutes, still inside the cake ring. If you are baking individual cookies, bake for 10 minutes. Both the cookie base and the individual cookies should have golden edges and a soft center.

7. Unmold the cookie(s): If you are making a cookie base, let it cool completely in the cake ring on the sheet pan. Once cooled, remove the cake ring. If you are baking individual cookies, let them cool until warm and then enjoy.

STORAGE

The cookie(s) can be stored in an airtight container or on a sheet pan wrapped in plastic wrap at room temperature for up to 2 days. Unbaked cookie dough can be wrapped tightly in plastic wrap and stored in the refrigerator for up to 5 days.

PAIR IT WITH

> **RECOMMENDED FILLINGS:** pastry cream, mousse, whipped ganache, caramel

> **RECOMMENDED FINISHINGS:** buttercreams, glaze, nappage glaze, Chantilly cream, ice cream

TWO IDEAS TO GET YOU STARTED

> As a mousse cake: Cookie Base (page 76) with Peanut Butter Mousse (page 195) then a layer of Chocolate Cake (page 22) and to finish Dark Chocolate Glaze (page 230)

> As an ice cream sandwich: Fruit Swirl Ice Cream (page 277) sandwiched between two individual cookies

SHOWSTOPPER

CHOCOLATE CHIP COOKIE COCONUT CAKE (page 182): Cookie Base (page 76) topped with a layer of Coconut Whipped Ganache (page 181), then a layer of Chocolate Cake (page 22), finished with Italian Meringue (page 258)

FLEUR DE SEL COOKIE BASE

MY GO-TO COOKIE BASE

A pinch of salt goes a long way in desserts. It brings out flavors you wouldn't otherwise detect—that caramel now tastes more buttery, that dough now nuttier. It can even make certain fruits taste sweeter (I like it with pineapple). But my favorite application is salt on a cookie.

THE CHANGE

In step 5 of **My Go-To Cookie Base** (page 76), sprinkle the unbaked cookie cake base or individual cookies with **2 grams (½ teaspoon) fleur de sel**, then bake as directed.

TWO IDEAS TO GET YOU STARTED

> As a mousse cake: Fleur de Sel Cookie Base (above) with Caramel Mousse (page 194) and Caramel Nappage Glaze (page 227)

> As a sandwich cookie: Chocolate Buttercream (page 222) sandwiched between two individual cookies

SPICED OR HERBED COOKIE BASE

Spices and herbs are an unexpected addition to your cookie base.

THE CHANGE

In step 3 of **My Go-To Cookie Base** (page 76), whisk **10 grams (3¾ teaspoons) ground cinnamon or 2 grams (2 teaspoons) ground culinary-grade lavender** into the dry ingredients. Proceed with the recipe as directed.

TWO IDEAS TO GET YOU STARTED

> As a cake: Lavender Cookie Base (above) with Blackberry Pastry Cream (page 125) then a layer of Almond Cake (page 34), and topped with Chantilly Cream (page 252)

> As a sandwich cookie: Soft Caramel (page 208) sandwiched between two individual Cinnamon Cookies

CHOCOLATE CHIP OR WALNUT COOKIE BASE

MY GO-TO COOKIE BASE

Flavor the dough for My Go-To Cookie Base with ingredients like chocolate chips and chopped walnuts.

THE CHANGE

In step 4 of **My Go-To Cookie Base** (page 76), make the dough as directed, then fold in **50 grams (⅓ cup) milk chocolate or dark chocolate chips*** or **50 grams (½ cup) chopped toasted walnuts*** with a spatula until evenly distributed. Proceed as directed in the recipe.

* *I like using a combination of milk chocolate and dark chocolate chips to give the cookies a more complex flavor.*

* *To toast walnuts, spread whole walnuts over a parchment paper–lined sheet pan and toast in a preheated 350°F (175°C) oven until golden in color, 3 to 4 minutes. Let cool completely, then coarsely chop.*

TWO IDEAS TO GET YOU STARTED

> As a cake: Chocolate Chip Cookie Base (above) decorated with piped Chocolate Buttercream (page 222) rosettes
> As an ice cream sandwich (page 81): Vanilla Ice Cream (page 274) sandwiched between two individual chocolate chip cookies

ROSEMARY CARAMEL BROWNIE
BASE: Rosemary-Infused Chocolate Brownies (page 88)
FILLING: Soft Caramel (page 208)
FINISHING: Sea salt

MY GO-TO CHOCOLATE BROWNIES

I fell in love with brownies when I moved to America. My favorite pieces are the corner edges—I love how the top crunches at the first bite, yielding to a chewy middle. You don't often find this combination in French pastries.

Like a chocolate chip cookie, people have preferences when it comes to brownies—they'll either seek the soft, gooey center pieces or the chewy edges. This recipe gives you the best of both.

These brownies are delicious on their own, but also make a terrific base for a mousse cake.

MAKES: 16 (2-inch or 5 cm) individual brownies or one 8-inch (20 cm) round cake base (2 to 2½ inches or 5 to 6.25 cm tall)
TIME: 45 minutes

INGREDIENTS

150 grams	1⅓ sticks	unsalted butter, at room temperature
300 grams	1½ cups	granulated sugar
135 grams	3 large	eggs
70 grams	½ cup + 4 teaspoons	cocoa powder, plus more for the pan
3 grams	½ teaspoon	salt
4 grams	1 teaspoon	baking powder
115 grams	1 cup	all-purpose flour
225 grams	8 ounces (1⅓ cups)	chocolate chips*

* *I like using milk chocolate chips for this recipe, but you could use dark chocolate instead, or a combination of the two.*

EQUIPMENT

8-inch (20 cm) square cake pan or 8-inch (20 cm) round cake pan

1. Preheat the oven: Preheat the oven to 350°F (175°C). Butter the bottom, sides, and edges of an 8-inch (20 cm) square or round cake pan. Pour in some cocoa powder and shake it around until the pan is evenly coated, then tap out any excess cocoa powder.*

* *Using cocoa powder instead of flour to dust your baking pan means there won't be any spots of white flour on the brownies when you remove them from the pan.*

2. Make the sugar mixture: Combine the butter and 100 grams (½ cup) of the sugar in a medium saucepan. Heat over medium heat, stirring slowly, until the sugar has dissolved and the butter has melted completely, 1 to 2 minutes.

3. Make the egg mixture: Whisk together the eggs and remaining 200 grams (1 cup) sugar until smooth.

4. Make the batter: Pour the sugar mixture into the egg mixture and whisk to combine. Add the cocoa powder, salt, baking powder, and flour and whisk to combine.* Add the chocolate chips and fold them in with a spatula until evenly incorporated. Pour the batter into the prepared pan until it reaches halfway up the sides. If you are making a cake base, pour it into the round cake pan. If you are making individual brownies, pour it into a square baking pan. Level the surface with a spatula if needed.

> * *Here's an easy way to sift dry ingredients: Combine them in a bowl and use a whisk to break up any lumps before adding them to a batter.*

5. Bake the brownie: Bake for 30 to 35 minutes. Because of their dark color, it's harder to tell when brownies are ready to come out of the oven. Look for the top of the brownies to set, with a few cracks in the surface.

6. Unmold the brownie: If you baked the brownie in a cake ring, let it cool completely in the ring on the sheet pan, then unmold it by pulling up the cake ring. If you are making individual brownies, let them cool for 15 to 20 minutes until they are warm and set, then cut them into squares and serve. I like to remove the corner square first to make the other squares easier to get out.

STORAGE

Brownies are best enjoyed the same day they're baked, but can be stored in an airtight container at room temperature for up to 2 days.

PAIR IT WITH

> Sometimes all you need is a glass of milk.

> **RECOMMENDED FILLINGS:** mousse, whipped ganache, caramel

> **RECOMMENDED FINISHINGS:** buttercream glaze, Chantilly cream, ice cream

TWO IDEAS TO GET YOU STARTED

> As a mousse cake: Dark Chocolate Champagne Mousse (page 204) with Dark Chocolate Glaze (page 230). For rich bases like this one, I prefer to build a lighter cake—like a mousse cake—rather than a layer cake.

> À la mode: top an individual brownie with a scoop of Vanilla Ice Cream (page 274) and a few spoonfuls of Dark Chocolate Ganache (page 137)

SHOWSTOPPER

CHOCOLATE CHERRY CAKE (page 164): Brownie base filled with Cherry Jam (page 163) and finished with Chocolate Buttercream (page 222) and fresh cherries (page 248)

SALTED PEANUT BUTTER CHOCOLATE BROWNIES

MY GO-TO CHOCOLATE BROWNIES

There are certain flavors that always work perfectly together. Peanut and chocolate are two. Enough said.

THE CHANGE

In step 4 of **My Go-To Chocolate Brownies** (page 84), after adding the chocolate chips, fold in **250 grams (1 cup) peanut butter*** with a spatula until just incorporated, leaving a few swirls. Pour the batter into the pan as directed, then sprinkle the surface with 3 grams (½ teaspoon) Maldon salt. Proceed with the recipe as directed; note that the peanut butter also adds moisture to the batter, so you may need to bake the brownies for 5 or so minutes more.

> * *I like using creamy peanut butter for this recipe, but you can use crunchy if you prefer. The peanut butter must be at room temperature to fold easily into your brownie batter. If you've just pulled it from the refrigerator, warm it in the microwave for a few seconds before adding it to the batter.*

TWO IDEAS TO GET YOU STARTED

> > As a cake: Go-To Vanilla Mousse (page 190)
> > À la mode: Serve with a big scoop of Chocolate Ice Cream (page 276).

ROSEMARY-INFUSED CHOCOLATE BROWNIES

BASE

MY GO-TO CHOCOLATE BROWNIES

Infuse fresh rosemary into the melted butter to give the brownies that extra little something. Remember: When working with herbs, a little goes a long way.

ADDED EQUIPMENT
Fine-mesh sieve

THE CHANGE

1. Strip the leaves from 2 grams coarsely chopped rosemary (1 tablespoon, about 5 sprigs).

2. In step 1 of **My Go-To Chocolate Brownies** (page 84), put the butter in a medium saucepan, but do not add the **100 grams (½ cup) sugar** yet. Melt the butter over medium heat. Remove from the heat and whisk in the rosemary. Cover the pan with a lid or plastic wrap and let stand for 30 minutes to infuse the butter with the flavor of the rosemary. Strain the butter through a fine-mesh sieve; discard the rosemary.

3. Return the butter to the saucepan and add the 100 grams (½ cup) sugar. Heat over medium heat, stirring slowly, until the sugar has dissolved, 1 to 2 minutes. Proceed with the recipe as directed.

TWO IDEAS TO GET YOU STARTED

> As a cake: Buttercream (page 220)
> Pour Soft Caramel (page 208) over the pan of brownies; let cool completely before slicing

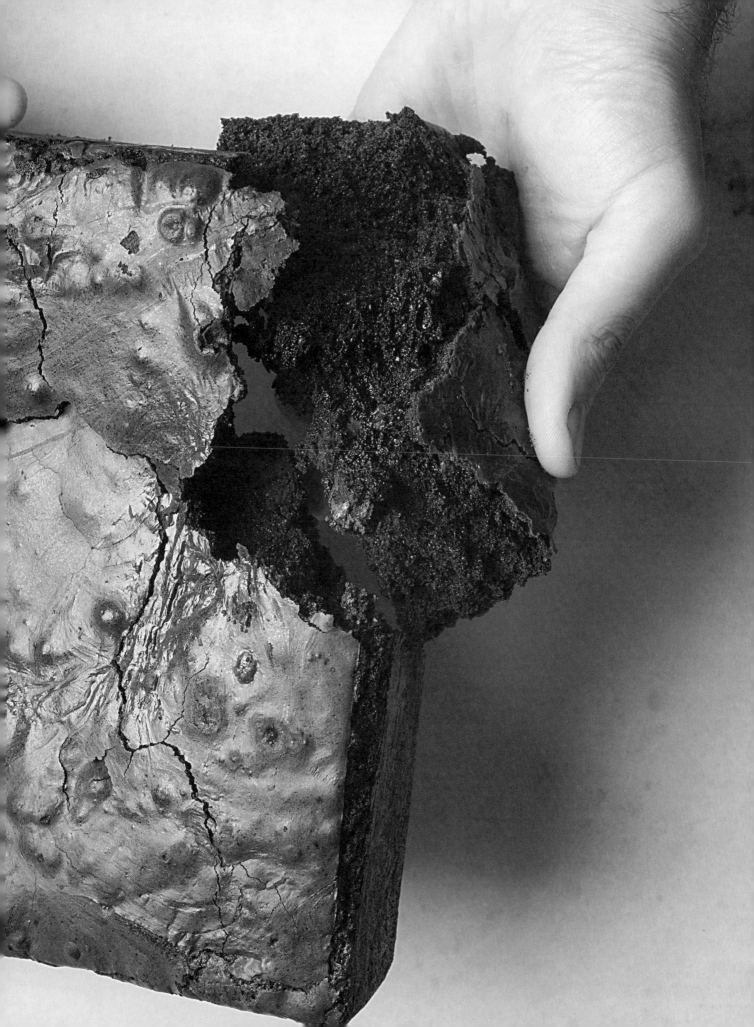

MY GO-TO SABLÉ BRETON

Think of this as a French shortbread. Sablé Breton is a crumbly, tender, salted butter cookie from Brittany. I use it as a base for fruit tarts—it's slightly thicker than a tart shell, and sturdier, too. Nothing is better than a sablé Breton topped with caramelized apples and a dollop of crème fraîche.

MAKES: One 8-inch (20 cm) cake base or 6 to 8 cookies
TIME: 2 hours 30 minutes

INGREDIENTS

65 grams	4 large	egg yolks
130 grams	⅔ cup	granulated sugar
125 grams	9 tablespoons	unsalted butter, very soft
175 grams	1½ cups	all-purpose flour, plus more for dusting
11 grams	2⅓ teaspoons	baking powder
1 gram	¼ teaspoon	fleur de sel

EQUIPMENT

Stand mixer with whisk attachment
8-inch (20 cm) cake ring*
Silicone baking mat (or parchment paper)

> * For this recipe, I prefer to use a cake ring (with no bottom) rather than a cake pan, as it's easier to unmold the sablé from a cake ring.

1. **Make the egg mixture:** In a stand mixer fitted with the whisk attachment (or in a large bowl using a hand mixer), combine the egg yolks and sugar and whip on high speed until light and fluffy, about 2 to 3 minutes. Add the butter and whip until fully incorporated.

2. **Add the dry ingredients:** Add the flour, baking powder, and fleur de sel to the mixer bowl and gently fold with a spatula until just combined.

3. **Chill the dough:** Turn the dough out onto a large piece of plastic wrap and gently form it into a ball. Wrap the dough in the plastic wrap. Refrigerate until firm, about 2 hours. (At this point, the dough can be refrigerated for later use—see Storage.)

4. **Preheat the oven:** Preheat the oven to 350°F (175°C). Line a sheet pan with a silicone baking mat or parchment paper.

5. Shape the dough: Dust your work surface with flour. For a cake base, dust an 8-inch (20 cm) cake ring with flour. Roll out the dough to ½ inch (1.5 cm) thick, then use the floured cake ring to punch out a disc of dough. Transfer the disc of dough, still in the cake ring, to the prepared sheet pan. For individual cookies, roll out the dough to ¼ inch (6 mm) thick, then use a round cookie cutter to punch out cookies. Place the cookies on the prepared sheet pan spaced at least 3 inches apart, as the dough will spread.

6. Bake the cake base or cookie(s): Bake the cake base or cookie(s) until golden brown all over, about 20 minutes. The dough will puff up slightly in the oven—that's okay.

7. Unmold the cake base or cookie(s): Let the cake base cool completely in the cake ring, then unmold by pulling the cake ring up and gently pushing down the cake base. Let the individual cookies cool on the sheet pan.

STORAGE

The sablé cake base and cookies can be stored in an airtight container at room temperature for up to 2 days.

The unbaked dough can be wrapped tightly in plastic wrap and stored in the refrigerator for up to 5 days or in the freezer for up to 2 weeks.

PAIR IT WITH

> **RECOMMENDED FILLINGS:** pastry cream, mousse, whipped ganache

> **RECOMMENDED FINISHINGS:** glaze

TWO IDEAS TO GET YOU STARTED

> As a cake: Topped with Caramelized Apples (page 240), with a dollop of crème fraîche on the side

> Dip individual cookies into Lemon Curd (page 134)

SHOWSTOPPER

BAKED APPLE ALMOND FRANGIPANE TART (page 95): Sablé Breton cake base filled with Almond Frangipane (page 123) and finished with Caramelized Apples (page 240)

BAKED ALMOND FRANGIPANE TART

There's a few times when you don't blind bake a tart shell. One of those times is when you are working with frangipane. Because frangipane contains eggs, it needs to be baked together with the (raw) tart shell.

1. Line the tart ring with the tart shell of choice. I love making an almond frangipane tart with my Go-To Sablé Breton (page 91), which can be thicker and crumblier than the regular Go-To Vanilla Sablé Tart Shell (page 4), but you can use either.

2. Fill the unbaked tart shell with a layer of Almond Frangipane (page 123) until it reaches halfway up the side of the tart shell. The almond frangipane will double in volume once baked so you don't want it to overflow. You can use a piping bag to fill the tart shell for more accuracy.

3. Top the almond frangipane with fresh, thinly sliced apples or pears. Nestle the fruit into the almond frangipane and fan them out evenly. Sprinkle a bit of cinnamon sugar on top prior to baking to caramelize the fruit.

4. Bake at 350°F (175°C) for 20 to 30 minutes until the tart shell is golden.

For a different take, omit the fresh fruit and bake the tart as directed. Then once baked, top with thicker wedges of Caramelized Apples (page 240), which can have a cleaner and more fruit-forward look for your tart.

APPLE ALMOND FRANGIPANE TART
BASE: Sablé Breton (page 91)
FILLING: Baked Almond Frangipane (page 123)
FINISHING: Caramelized Apples (page 240)
TECHNIQUE: Baked Almond Frangipane Tart (page 93)

CHOCOLATE SABLÉ BRETON

BASE

MY GO-TO SABLÉ BRETON

Transform My Go-To Sablé Breton into a chocolate sablé by simply adding cocoa powder to the dry ingredients. The cocoa powder adds richness, which results in a chocolatey, yet still crumbly, cookie.

THE CHANGE

In step 2 of **My Go-To Sablé Breton** (page 91), add **75 grams (⅔ cup) unsweetened cocoa powder** to the mixer bowl when you add the flour.* Proceed with the recipe as directed.

> * *If you're making a cake base, use cocoa powder instead of flour to dust the cake ring, too, to avoid white patches on your finished dessert.*

TWO IDEAS TO GET YOU STARTED

> As a cake: Banana Pastry Cream (page 125) with Caramelized Bananas (page 238)

> Dip individual cookies into Cherry Dark Chocolate Ganache (page 143)

HAZELNUT SABLÉ BRETON

MY GO-TO SABLÉ BRETON

Toasted hazelnuts add a nutty flavor and smell—as well as some crunch—to the sablé. Toasted almonds, peanuts, or walnuts would also work well here.

THE CHANGE

After adding the dry ingredients in step 2 of **My Go-To Sablé Breton** (page 91), add **50 grams (½ cup) chopped toasted* blanched (skinless) hazelnuts** and gently fold them in with a spatula until evenly incorporated.* Proceed with the recipe as directed.

* To toast your hazelnuts, coarsely chop whole hazelnuts and spread them out on a parchment-lined cookie sheet. Toast in a preheated 350°F (175°C) oven for 10 to 15 minutes, until they've browned lightly and you can smell their toasted nutty aroma.

* If you prefer, sprinkle the toasted nuts on top of the unbaked cookie base or cookies rather than incorporating them into the dough.

TWO IDEAS TO GET YOU STARTED

> As a cake: Kahlúa Dark Chocolate Ganache (page 144) with Caramel Glaze (page 227)

> Dip individual cookies into Orange Curd (page 136)

MY GO-TO CARAMELIZED PUFFED RICE

I love slowly caramelized puffed rice as a crunchy base for layer cakes. That crispy contrast works particularly well in creamy mousse- and ganache-based cakes.

MAKES: One 8-inch (20 cm) cake base
TIME: 15 minutes

INGREDIENTS

70 grams	2 cups	puffed rice
35 grams	2 tablespoons	light corn syrup
18 grams	1 tablespoon + ¾ teaspoon	granulated sugar

EQUIPMENT

Silicone baking mat (or parchment paper)
8-inch (20 cm) cake ring

1. Preheat the oven: Preheat the oven to 350°F (175°C). Line a sheet pan with a silicone baking mat or parchment paper and set an 8-inch (20 cm) cake ring in the pan.

2. Coat the puffed rice: Put the puffed rice in a large bowl. Put the corn syrup in a small heatproof bowl and microwave for 30 seconds, then pour the warm corn syrup over the puffed rice. Sprinkle with the sugar, then mix with a spatula until the rice is evenly coated. (You may find that using your hands is easier.)

3. Shape puffed rice: Transfer the puffed rice to the cake ring, pressing it into an even layer about ¼ inch (6 mm) thick. If you plan on using the caramelized puffed rice as a topping, separate it into clusters on a sheet pan.

4. Bake the puffed rice: Bake for 10 to 15 minutes, until golden brown and caramelized.

5. Unmold the puffed rice: Let the puffed rice cool completely in the cake ring. Unmold the puffed rice, then carefully peel away the silicone mat or parchment.

STORAGE

The caramelized puffed rice can be stored in an airtight container in a cool, dry place for up to 1 week.

TWO IDEAS TO GET YOU STARTED

> On its own: Sprinkle carmalized puffed rice on top of Ice Cream (page 274) or on Roasted Fruits (page 246)

> As a sandwich cookie: Carmalized puffed rice sandwiched with Passion Fruit curd (page 136)

SHOWSTOPPER

PEANUT BUTTER CRUNCH CAKE (page 103): Caramelized Puffed Rice Base filled with Peanut Butter Mousse (page 195) and finished with Dark Chocolate Ganache (page 137)

CHOCOLATE OR PEANUT BUTTER CARAMELIZED PUFFED RICE

BASE

MY GO-TO CARAMELIZED PUFFED RICE

Coat your caramelized puffed rice with a layer of milk or dark chocolate—or even creamy peanut butter.

THE CHANGE

1. Prepare **My Go-To Caramelized Puffed Rice** as directed on page 100.

2. For **chocolate puffed rice**, put **70 grams (2½ ounces) milk chocolate or dark chocolate** in a heatproof bowl. Microwave in 10- to 15-second intervals, stirring after each, until just melted—don't let it get too hot. For **peanut butter puffed rice**, put **60 grams (¼ cup) creamy peanut butter** in a heatproof bowl and microwave in 30-second intervals, stirring after each, until fluid. Put **60 grams ½ ounce white chocolate** in a separate heatproof bowl. Microwave in 30-second intervals, stirring after each, until just melted—don't let it get too hot. Fold the white chocolate into the peanut butter until incorporated.

3. Line a sheet pan or an 8-inch (20 cm) cake pan with parchment paper. Place the disc of puffed rice in a large bowl. With your hands, break it into smaller pieces. Pour the melted chocolate or peanut butter over the puffed rice and fold with a spatula until coated.

4. Spread the coated puffed rice over the prepared sheet pan or press it into the prepared cake pan. Refrigerate until firm, about 20 minutes.

5. Gently unmold the puffed rice and remove the parchment. (Work quickly, or the chocolate will melt.)

TWO IDEAS TO GET YOU STARTED

> As a cake: Chocolate Puffed Rice cake base with Vanilla Mousse (page 90), then a layer of Chocolate Cake (page 22)

> As a sandwich cookie: Peanut Butter Puffed Rice (above) sandwiched with Soft Caramel (page 208) sprinkled with sea salt

EVERYONE CAN BAKE

102

MY GO-TO BAKED VANILLA MERINGUE (FOR A PAVLOVA)

Pavlovas are among the most popular desserts at my bakeries. A pavlova has a wonderful mix of textures: with its crunchy shell and soft center, the meringue is a perfect base for sweet cream and tart fruits.

MAKES: One 4-inch (10 cm) meringue
TIME: 45 minutes to 1 hour

INGREDIENTS

135 grams	1 cup	confectioners' sugar
65 grams	2 large	egg whites

EQUIPMENT

Stand mixer with whisk attachment (I don't recommend doing this by hand)
Digital thermometer
4-inch (10 cm) ring mold with 2-inch (5 cm) sides
Silicone baking mat (or parchment paper)

1. **Preheat the oven:** Preheat the oven to 375°F (190°C). Line a sheet pan with a silicone baking mat or parchment paper and set a 4-inch (10 cm) ring mold with 2-inch (5 cm) sides in the pan.

2. **Make the egg white mixture:** In a stand mixer fitted with the whisk attachment, combine the confectioners' sugar and egg whites and whip on low speed until combined.

3. Fill a large saucepan with about 3 inches (7.5 cm) of water and bring to a simmer over medium heat.* Clip a digital thermometer to the side of the mixer bowl and set the bowl over the pan of simmering water. Heat the egg white mixture, whisking continuously, until it reaches 113°F (45°C).* Remove from the heat.*

   * *Make sure the bottom of the bowl doesn't touch the simmering water; otherwise, the egg whites might scramble.*

   * *It's important to use a thermometer for making meringues as it needs to be precisely monitored.*

* *This a Swiss meringue, a type of meringue that's cooked twice—first when it's heated over simmering water, then when it's baked in the oven. The meringue will have a thin, crunchy exterior, but depending on how long you bake it, the interior can either be crunchy throughout or soft and moist.*

4. Make the meringue: Return the mixer bowl to the stand mixer. Whip the warm egg white mixture on high speed until it holds stiff peaks, 5 to 7 minutes. The meringue should be fluffy and tripled in volume.

5. Shape the meringue: Using a spatula, scoop the meringue into the ring mold,* smoothing it with a spatula to fill the edges. Carefully remove the ring mold.

   * *If you don't have a ring mold, you can use a spatula to form the meringue into a 4-inch (10 cm) disc about 2 inches (5 cm) thick.*

6. Bake the meringue: Bake for 10 minutes, then decrease the oven temperature to 325°F (163°C) and bake for 20 minutes more, until the outside of the meringue is crisp and golden blond in color but the inside is still soft. The meringue will spread slightly as it bakes.

7. Let cool: Let the meringue cool completely on the sheet pan (and be careful not to touch it much, as it might deflate).

STORAGE

The meringue is best enjoyed the same day it's baked, but can be wrapped in plastic wrap and stored at room temperature for up to 2 days.

TWO IDEAS TO GET YOU STARTED

> Vanilla Chantilly Cream (page 252) and fresh raspberries (page 248)
> Passion Fruit Curd (page 136) and fresh strawberries (page 248)

SHOWSTOPPERS

GRAPEFRUIT TARRAGON PAVLOVA (page 128): Italian Meringue (page 258)filled with Grapefruit Curd (page 136) and finished with Tarragon Chantilly Cream (page 253), fresh grapefruit (page 248), and Nappage Glaze (page 223)

BLACKBERRY LEMON VERBENA PAVLOVA: Italian Meringue (Baked) (page 258) filled with Blackberry Jam (page 159) and Lemon Verbena Chiboust (page 127) and finished with fresh blackberries (page 248)

FLAVORED BAKED MERINGUE

BASE

MY GO-TO BAKED VANILLA MERINGUE

Flavor the meringue for a pavlova with ingredients like nut butters, fresh herbs, or cocoa powder, by following the steps below.

THE CHANGE

In step 4 of **My Go-To Baked Vanilla Meringue** (page 106), whip the meringue until it holds stiff peaks, then flavor as desired:

> For **nut butter meringue**, put **15 grams (1 tablespoon) almond butter or peanut butter** in a medium bowl. Add a scoop of the meringue to the nut butter and gently fold until combined, then transfer the nut butter mixture to the bowl with the remaining meringue and fold gently with a spatula until just incorporated.*

> * *Always fold gently and carefully so as not to deflate the meringue.*

> For **fresh herb meringue**, add the finely chopped leaves of **1 sprig fresh mint or basil*** and fold gently with a spatula until just incorporated.

> * *Other herbs that work well with fresh fruits include lemon thyme and tarragon.*

> For **chocolate meringue**, sift **20 grams (2¾ tablespoons) cocoa powder** into a medium bowl. Add a scoop of the meringue and gently fold until well combined, then transfer the cocoa mixture to the bowl with the remaining meringue and fold gently with a spatula until just incorporated.*

> * *If you want swirls of cocoa in your meringue, on the last few folds hold back so that you still retain the separation of the cocoa stripes from the meringue.*

Proceed with the recipe as directed.

THREE IDEAS TO GET YOU STARTED

> With the Almond Butter Meringue: Greek Yogurt Chantilly Cream (page 253) with Roasted Figs

> With the Mint Meringue: Orange Curd (page 136) with Orange Slices

> With the Chocolate Meringue: Chestnut-Whiskey Chantilly Cream (page 253) with a drizzle of Dark Chocolate Ganache (page 137)

MY GO-TO PÂTE À CHOUX

Chances are you've eaten plenty of things made with pâte à choux—éclairs or profiteroles or cream puffs. This egg-based dough is best filled with custard, pastry cream, or whipped ganache. I like mine filled with coconut whipped ganache and lemon curd because the nuttiness of the coconut mellows the creamy curd.

MAKES: 30 profiteroles, 15 éclairs, or 1 Paris-Brest
TIME: 1 hour

INGREDIENTS

75 grams	⅓ cup	water
70 grams	¼ cup + 1 teaspoon	whole milk
75 grams	5½ tablespoons	unsalted butter
3 grams	1 teaspoon	granulated sugar
2 grams	1 teaspoon	salt
100 grams	⅔ cup	all-purpose flour
150 to 200 grams	3 to 4 large	eggs
20 grams	1 large	egg yolk

EQUIPMENT

Stand mixer with the paddle attachment
Piping bag fitted with large round plain tip (at least ⅓ inch/1 cm opening)
Pastry brush

1. Preheat the oven: Preheat the oven to 375°F (190°C). Line a sheet pan with parchment paper. For éclairs, use a ruler to measure out 5 inches (13 cm) so you have a guideline for piping the eclairs. For choux rings for Paris-Brest, place an 8-inch (20 cm) cake ring or pan on the parchment and use it as a guide to draw a circle on the parchment with a marker. Flip the parchment ink-side down.

2. Make the dough: Combine the water, milk, butter, sugar, and salt in a medium saucepan and bring to a boil over medium heat, stirring occasionally. Add in the flour and stir vigorously with a spatula until a dough comes together, 1 to 2 minutes. Cook, stirring, until a film starts to form at the bottom of the saucepan as the result of the dough sticking, 1 to 2 minutes. Keep going until the white film completely covers the bottom of the pan, which should take about 5 more minutes. Remove from the heat.

3. Add the eggs: Transfer the dough to the bowl of a stand mixer fitted with a paddle attachment. Mix on low speed for about 5 minues. When making pâte à choux, the amount of eggs needed will vary. The consistency of the dough dictates how many eggs should be added. Sometimes the dough dries out a bit more in the pan and can take on more eggs.* With the mixer on low speed, paddle the dough to let off some heat and steam, and then begin to add the eggs one at a time, mixing until each egg is fully incorporated before adding the next one. You'll add 150 to 200 grams of eggs (3 to 4 eggs). The outside of the bowl should be hot to the touch, but bearable.

 * *To check, stick a spatula into the dough and lift it high above the bowl. The dough should fall slowly off the spatula in ribbons. It should feel thick, but fluid enough to pipe.*

4. Shape the dough: Using a spatula, place two large scoops of the choux dough into a piping bag fitted with a large plain tip, filling it one-third full. Push the dough down toward the tip of the bag. Pipe the dough into the desired shape, refilling the bag as necessary until you have used all the dough. (See page 312 to learn piping techniques.)

 > **For cream puffs or profiteroles:** Holding the piping bag at a 90-degree angle about ½ inch (1.25 cm) above the prepared sheet pan, pipe rounds of choux dough about 1½ inches (4 cm) in diameter, spacing them about 1 inch (3.5 cm) apart. Smooth/flatten the pointed tips of the rounds with your fingers.

 > **For éclairs:** Pipe 5-inch (13 cm) long eclairs that are spaced at least 1 inch (2.5 cm) apart.

 > **For choux rings or Paris-Brest:** Using the marker circle as a guide, pipe a ring of choux onto the prepared pan, then pipe another ring directly inside the first (they should be touching). Then pipe a third ring on top of the first two on top.

5. Brush with egg wash: Beat together the remaining 50 grams (1) egg and the egg yolk in a small bowl. Using a pastry brush or the tips of your fingers, lightly brush the egg wash over the choux.

6. Bake the choux: Bake the choux on the center rack until golden brown, light to the touch, and hollow when broken open, rotating the pan 180 degrees halfway through the baking time.

 > Bake **cream puffs or profiteroles** for 20 to 25 minutes.
 > Bake **éclairs** for 20 to 25 minutes.
 > Bake **choux rings or Paris-Brest** for 25 to 30 minutes.

7. Unmold the choux: Let the choux cool completely in the pan, then gently remove them from the parchment and fill as desired.

STORAGE

Filled choux are best eaten right away, but can be stored in an airtight container in the refrigerator for up to 1 day.

PAIR IT WITH

> **RECOMMENDED FILLINGS:** pastry cream, curd, jam, whipped ganache

> **RECOMMENDED FINISHINGS:** Chantilly cream, fresh fruit, glaze

TWO IDEAS TO GET YOU STARTED

> Coconut Whipped Ganache (page 181) and Passion Fruit Curd (page 136), sprinkled with confectioners' sugar

> Pastry Cream with Dark Chocolate Ganache (page 137)

SHOWSTOPPER

RASPBERRY CREAM PUFF CAKE: Choux Ring with Profiterole Top, filled with Raspberry Jam (page 159) and finished with fresh raspberries (page 248) and Vanilla Chantilly Cream (page 252)

FILLINGS

If the base is the *identity* of the dessert, then the filling is its *personality*.

Bases determine texture: a chewy cookie base or a flaky tart shell. Fillings amplify flavor. You will never get a deep, dark, complex chocolate flavor from a chocolate cake alone. It needs a filling to really deliver, to determine if that chocolate cake will be demure (add a soft mascarpone or vanilla filling), classic (add a tried-and-true pastry cream), or adventurous (add exotic fruits, nuts, or herb- or floral-infused fillings). And using too many ingredients or flavors can make the personality of the cake become confused—you need a point of view.

Sometimes the flavors blend seamlessly and form one harmonious chord—chocolate and caramel work hand in hand, for example; lavender and honey do, too. Other times one flavor is the star and is supported by accents that amplify it—bananas taste delicious with just a hint of cinnamon and clove, and strawberries shine brighter with a dash of balsamic vinegar.

Finding the right balance is more of an art than a science. Start with your favorites, then twist them and push the envelope with them, and once in a while, throw in a wild card idea.

Some combinations are included in this book, while others draw from flavors not mentioned here. My hope is that this will spark your creativity.

CLASSIC	WITH A TWIST	ADVENTUROUS

FRUIT

Orange–Brown Sugar	Orange–Lemon Thyme	Orange–Olive Oil
Peach-Mascarpone	Peach-Rosemary	Peach–Lemon Verbena
Apple-Caramel	Apple-Gingerbread	Apple–Port Chocolate

CHOCOLATE

All Dark Chocolate	Chocolate-Hazelnut	Dark Chocolate–Basil
Milk Chocolate–Peanut Butter	Milk Chocolate–Earl Grey	Milk Chocolate–Lavender
White Chocolate–Strawberry	White Chocolate–Lemon	White Chocolate–Matcha

NUTS & SPICES

All Vanilla	Vanilla-Honey	Vanilla-Lavender
Hazelnut-Espresso	Hazelnut-Blackberry	Hazelnut-Coconut
Cinnamon-Banana	Cinnamon-Pear	Cinnamon-Almond
Caramel-Salt	Caramel-Thyme	Caramel-Anise

MY GO-TO PASTRY CREAM

There's something about a pastry cream that no mousse or ganache can ever replicate. It's smooth and custardy—the perfect texture. You can eat it on its own by the spoonful almost like pudding, but it's terrific in tarts and on cakes. It's sturdy enough not to collapse under the weight of fresh berries, and subtle in flavor, so it highlights even the most delicate fruits.

MAKES: 1 kilogram (4 cups), enough to fill one 8-inch tart or one two-layered 8-inch or 20 cm cake, with leftover pastry cream*

TIME: 45 minutes

> * Top leftover pastry cream with fruit or streusel for an easy dessert or afternoon snack.

INGREDIENTS

535 grams	2¼ cups	whole milk
130 grams	⅔ cup	granulated sugar
50 grams	⅓ cup	cornstarch
185 grams	9 large	egg yolks
110 grams	8 tablespoons (1 stick)	unsalted butter, cut into cubes, at room temperature

EQUIPMENT
Fine-mesh sieve

1. Make the warm milk mixture: Combine the milk and 65 grams (⅓ cup) of the sugar in a medium saucepan. Bring to a boil over medium heat, whisking continuously. Remove from the heat.

2. Make the cornstarch mixture: Whisk together the remaining 65 grams (⅓ cup) sugar and the cornstarch in a large bowl. Slowly whisk in ½ cup of the warm milk mixture.

3. Temper the egg yolks: While whisking, add the egg yolks to the cornstarch mixture one at a time, whisking until each yolk is incorporated before adding the next.* Pour the tempered egg yolk mixture into the pan with the remaining milk mixture.

> * This technique is called tempering, and is used to gradually raise the temperature of a cold or room-temperature ingredient (in this case, egg yolks) by adding small amounts of warm liquid, to prevent the cold ingredient from cooking too quickly. If you added all the warm liquid to the eggs without tempering them first, you would end up with scrambled eggs.

4. Finish the pastry cream: Cook the pastry cream over medium-low heat, whisking continuously, until it thickens to a pudding-like consistency, about 5 minutes. Remove from the heat. Add the butter and whisk until the butter is evenly combined and the pastry cream is pale yellow with a smooth, glossy texture. Strain the pastry cream through a fine-mesh sieve to remove any lumps. Let cool and then chill before using.

STORAGE

The pastry cream can be stored in the refrigerator in an airtight container, with plastic wrap pressed against the surface of the pastry cream to prevent a skin from forming, for up to 3 days. Before using, stir the pastry cream with a spatula until it softens and is spreadable.

BEST FOR

> Anything in a tart shell
> Anything made with pâte à choux (like éclairs and cream puffs, to name a few!)

ALMOND FRANGIPANE

Almond Frangipane is an almond cream lightened with pastry cream, and it works well as a base for fruit tarts. I love Baked Almond Frangipane tarts (page 93): a layer of almond frangipane piped into a tart shell, topped with tender slices of poached pears, then baked until golden.

MAKES: 750 grams (3 cups), enough to fill one 8-inch tart or one two-layered 8-inch or 20 cm cake, with leftover almond frangipane*
TIME: 1 hour 30 minutes

> * *Extra almond frangipane can be used to fill leftover croissants, then soaked in sugar syrup to be baked into almond croissants.*

ALMOND CREAM

120 grams	8 tablespoons (1 stick)	unsalted butter, at room temperature
110 grams	¾ cup + 2 teaspoons	confectioners' sugar
100 grams	2 large	eggs, at room temperature
15 grams	1 tablespoon	rum
150 grams	1½ cups	almond flour

ADDED EQUIPMENT
Stand mixer with paddle attachment or hand mixer
Piping bag

THE CHANGE

1. Make the pastry cream: Prepare **My Go-To Pastry Cream** (page 121) as directed. Let cool completely, then press a piece of plastic wrap directly against the surface of the pastry cream and refrigerate while you make the almond cream.

2. Make the almond cream: In a stand mixer fitted with the paddle attachment (or in a large bowl using a hand mixer), beat the butter on medium speed until light and fluffy, 2 to 3 minutes. Add the confectioners' sugar and beat until incorporated. Add one egg and the rum, then beat until incorporated. Turn off the mixer and scrape down the sides of the bowl. Add the remaining egg and beat on medium speed until incorporated, then stop and scrape down the sides once more. Add the almond flour and beat until completely combined. Stop and scrape down the sides of the bowl once more.

3. Combine the pastry cream and almond cream: Remove the pastry cream from the refrigerator and mix with a spatula until spreadable. Combine 250 grams (1 cup) pastry cream and 500 grams (2 cups) almond cream in a large bowl and mix with a spatula until combined.

STORAGE

The almond frangipane can be stored in the refrigerator in an airtight container, with plastic wrap pressed against the surface of the almond frangipane to prevent a skin from forming, for up to 3 days. Because it contains raw eggs, it must be baked before being eaten.

FRUIT-FLAVORED PASTRY CREAM

FILLING

MY GO-TO PASTRY CREAM

Flavor basic pastry cream with fruit purées, such as the blackberry or banana I've suggested here. The flavor of fruit in the pastry creams are delicate, so you won't get that brightness or tartness of fresh fruit, but you'll capture a bit of its essence. Play up that delicateness by pairing it with soft whipped cream, in banana cream pie, for instance.

THE CHANGE

Prepare **My Go-To Pastry Cream** (page 121) as directed, then whisk in **145 grams (⅔ cup) blackberry purée or 215 grams (¾ cup) banana purée**.* Strain the pastry cream through a fine-mesh sieve to remove any lumps.

> * *Prepared blackberry purée and banana purée can be found in specialty stores and online. To make your own, in a blender, purée 145 grams (1 cup) fresh blackberries or 215 grams peeled ripe bananas (about 2 bananas) until smooth. Strain the blackberry purée through a fine-mesh sieve to remove the seeds.*

CHOCOLATE OR NUT PASTRY CREAM

FILLING

MY GO-TO PASTRY CREAM

Just as pastry cream can be pulled in the direction of fruit, it can also take on a richer persona by adding in chocolate or nut paste. Once mixed with pastry cream, the flavors will soften and become more subtle. If you love both fruit and chocolate, my tip is to always add the zest of half an orange to accentuate the chocolate or nutty flavors.

THE CHANGE

Prepare **My Go-To Pastry Cream** (page 121) as directed, then whisk in **75 grams (⅓ cup) hazelnut paste or peanut butter or dark chocolate (melted)**. Strain through a fine-mesh sieve to remove any lumps.

HERB-INFUSED PASTRY CREAM

To add herb flavors to your pastry cream, simply infuse the milk for My Go-To Pastry Cream. Any recipe with a decent amount of milk can have that milk take on flavor through an infusion, which works very much like the way you steep a cup of tea. I love the freshness of lemon verbena, but lavender and rose are also beautiful flavors.

ADDED EQUIPMENT

Fine-mesh sieve

THE CHANGE

In step 1 of **My Go-To Pastry Cream** (page 121), prepare the warm milk mixture as directed, then add **6 grams (5 tablespoons) dried lemon verbena, rose petals, or lavender**, cover with a lid or plastic wrap, and let stand for 15 minutes to infuse. Strain the mixture through a fine-mesh sieve and discard the solids. Proceed with the recipe as directed.

CHIBOUST

A chiboust is a pastry cream combined with Italian meringue, resulting in a lighter-textured cream.

MAKES: 1 kilogram (7 cups), enough to fill one 8-inch tart or one two-layered 8-inch or 20 cm cake, with leftover chiboust
TIME: 30 to 40 minutes (if pastry cream is already made)

INGREDIENTS

5 grams	1½ teaspoons + ⅛ teaspoon	unflavored powdered gelatin
25 grams	1 tablespoon + 2 teaspoons	cold water
	1 recipe	My Go-To Pastry Cream (page 121)
	1 recipe	My Go-To Vanilla Meringue (page 106)

THE CHANGE

1. Dissolve the gelatin: Combine the gelatin and cold water in a small bowl and stir with a spoon until the gelatin has dissolved.

2. Make the pastry cream: Prepare the pastry cream as directed. While the pastry cream is still warm, stir in the gelatin mixture with a spatula. Let the pastry cream cool completely, about 30 minutes.

3. Meanwhile, make the meringue: Prepare the meringue as directed and measure out 390 grams (3¼ cups); reserve the remainder for another use.

4. Finish the chiboust: Add 130 grams (about 1 cup) of the meringue to the pastry cream* and gently fold it in with a spatula to lighten the pastry cream. Gently fold in the rest of the meringue until combined. (Mix carefully so as not to deflate the meringue.) Use the chiboust immediately; refrigerating will cause the meringue to separate and deflate.

 * *If you made your pastry cream in advance and stored it in the refrigerator, remember to temper it first by bringing it out from the refrigerator and mixing it with a spatula to make it smooth and spreadable.*

HOW TO ADD FLAVOR TO YOUR CHIBOUST: You can flavor the chiboust in any direction by flavoring the pastry cream. For example, for a Lemon Verbena Chiboust, just make a Lemon Verbena Pastry Cream (page 126).

STORAGE

Chiboust should be used immediately; it cannot be stored for later use.

GRAPEFRUIT TARRAGON PAVLOVA
BASE: Italian Meringue (Baked) (page 258)
FILLING: Grapefruit Curd (page 136)
FINISHING: Tarragon Chantilly Cream + Fresh grapefruit (page 248)
+ Nappage Glaze (page 223)

Baking Is Like Jazz

Louis Armstrong once said, "We all do 'do, re, mi,' but you have got the find the other notes yourselves." His music plays softly in the background of our kitchen amid the sounds of scrubbing and cleaning at the end of a long day.

Chefs, like musicians, rely on established chords and compose with respect to them. And just like jazz musicians, we must first learn "do, re, mi" before finding the other notes ourselves.

As a young chef in France, I was handed recipes and told to replicate them. The chef walked around the kitchen in his tall toque, policing our work, his footsteps setting the pace like a metronome. The fluorescent ceiling light flickered as I squinted to read the recipes. I didn't always like the constraints of regimented directions, but I did like the unlimited inspirations I found in every bite I tasted. I kept a mental log of my favorite flavors and combinations: the soulful pairing of caramel and apples cooked down in Calvados; the refreshing blend of tart raspberry and delicate coconut. I remember baking, and tasting, a hazelnut-lemon cake for the first time: the two very different flavors blended perfectly—the combination was at once refreshing and decadent. Think of the way you would add lemon into iced tea—how the dark, bitter aromas of the tea work perfectly in harmony with the sour accents. I was learning the established harmonies and chords.

I didn't stay in France for long. The day I received my passport in the mail, my eighteen-year-old face staring back at me from the photo, the world—and all of its flavors—opened to me. I loved tasting everything as I traveled. I tried lemongrass in Bali and realized, for the first time, that ingredients other than citrus fruits could impart the same citrus flavor. I tried shiso in Japan, and in it, recognized the flavors of mint and basil on my tongue. I tried pink peppercorn on a smoked salmon carpaccio, and I understood that pepper could add brightness as well as heat to a dish. I memorized every flavor, and each new ingredient was an additional resource, a new song, a melody to keep in my repertoire. I traveled, I tasted, I played my jazz.

A few years ago, someone asked me what my favorite flavor was. I mentally flipped through my memories of exotic ingredients from around the world, remembering the taste of freshly cut pineapple in Martinique, its flesh so rich, it seemed like it had been candied; but I also found myself somewhere closer to home, recalling the taste of ripe apricots I had eaten in the South of France, their juices as complex and fragrant as honey wine. These flavors, and others I had catalogued in my mind, were unique to a particular place and season. When I realized I couldn't source these fruits in my kitchens in New

York, I began trying to re-create them. I added drops of rose water to mango to mimic the floral quality of Alphonso mangoes I had tried from India. To re-create the fresh passion fruit that I'd enjoyed in Hawaii, the fruit still warm from the sun, I sprinkled lychee juice over the passion fruit to pull back its tartness and round out its flavors.

Blending ingredients like a perfumer, and using them to enhance the perfect flavors I kept in my memory, became my go-to style—I had found my "sound." And this book, unlike those unchangeable recipes from my culinary past, gives you the opportunity to change, to adapt, to jazz up recipes and make them your own. You have to live a bit and experience a lot to find what's right for you.

Nina Simone once said, "Jazz is not just music. It's a way of life, it's a way of being, a way of thinking." So, too, with baking.

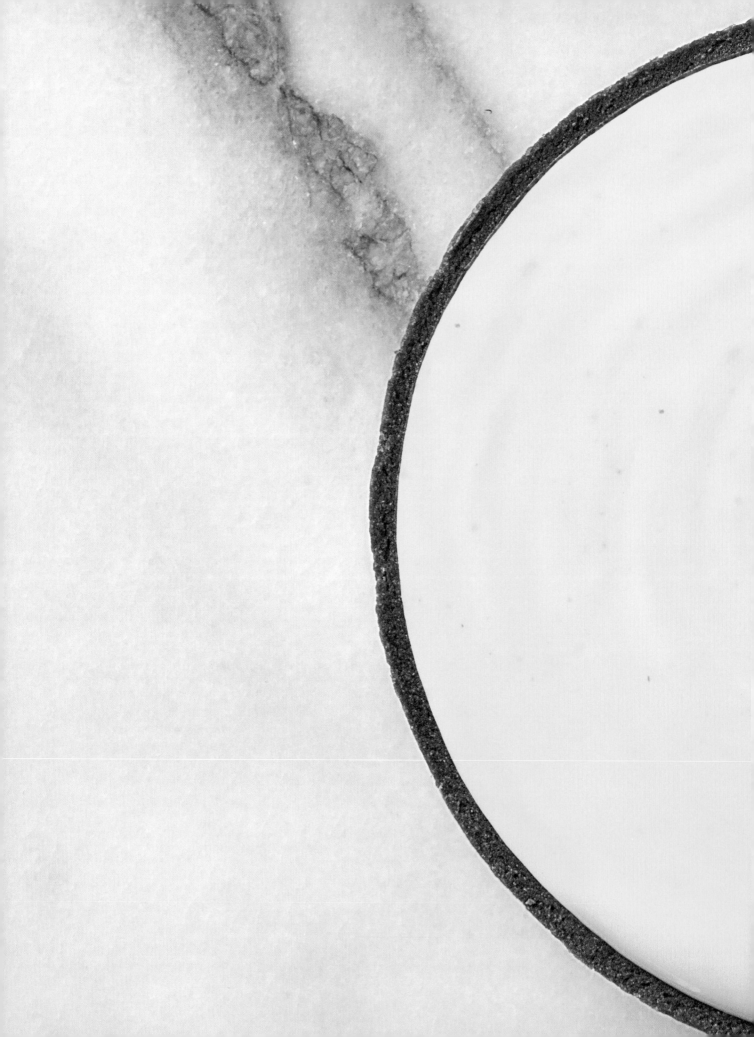

MY GO-TO
LEMON CURD

I don't like lemon curds that start out too tart and are only balanced by too much sugar. Two wrongs don't make a right. The perfect lemon curd is slightly tart and slightly sweet, buttery and smooth.

I love using Meyer lemons in this recipe; they're sweeter and more floral than traditional lemons. Their skin is so tender, you can eat it just as is or dipped in a bit of Dark Chocolate Ganache (page 137).

MAKES: 500 grams (2 cups), enough to fill one 8-inch tart or one two-layered 8-inch or 20 cm cake, with leftover lemon curd
TIME: 30 minutes

INGREDIENTS

3 grams	¾ teaspoon	unflavored powdered gelatin
12 grams	2¼ teaspoons	cold water
3 grams	1½ teaspoons	lemon zest
95 grams	6 tablespoons	fresh lemon juice*
115 grams	½ cup + 1 tablespoon	granulated sugar
160 grams	3 large	eggs
105 grams	8 tablespoons (1 stick)	unsalted butter, cut into cubes, at room temperature

* No need to use a messy juicer: Roll the lemon on your work surface, then slice it in half crosswise. Set a strainer over a small bowl to catch any seeds, then, holding a lemon half over the strainer, simply stick a fork into the fruit and twist gently to extract the juice.

1. **Dissolve the gelatin:** Combine the gelatin and water in a small bowl and stir with a spoon until the gelatin has dissolved.

2. **Make the curd base:** Combine the lemon zest, lemon juice, and sugar in a medium saucepan and bring to a simmer over medium heat, stirring until the sugar has dissolved. Remove from the heat.

3. **Temper the eggs:** Whisk the eggs in a large bowl. While whisking, pour one-quarter of the curd base into the eggs and whisk to combine. Repeat with another quarter of the curd mixture. Pour the tempered egg mixture into the saucepan with the remaining curd base and whisk until smooth and combined.

4. Cook the curd: Cook the curd over medium heat, stirring continuously, until it starts to bubble, then whisk in the gelatin mixture. Remove from the heat and let cool until just warm.

5. Finish the curd: Add the butter to the curd and whisk until the butter is fully incorporated and the curd is silky and smooth. Let cool completely before serving.

STORAGE

The lemon curd can be stored in the refrigerator in an airtight container, with plastic wrap pressed against the surface of the curd to prevent a skin from forming, for up to 4 days. Leftover lemon curd can be spread on toast or Sablé Breton (page 91) cookies.

BEST FOR

> Anything that needs a filling, from tarts and cakes to meringnes, you name it.

CITRUS CURDS

Once you perfect a basic lemon curd, you can experiment with different citrus flavors. Look for something that has a tartness to it—whether it's a fragrant passion fruit or a mellow orange.

THE CHANGE

For Passion Fruit Curd: In step 2 of **My Go-To Lemon Curd** (page 134), omit the lemon zest and replace the lemon juice with **95 grams (6 tablespoons) strained passion fruit juice**. Proceed with the recipe as directed.

For Orange Curd: Replace the lemon zest with **3 grams (1½ teaspoons) orange zest** and the lemon juice with **95 grams (6 tablespoons) strained fresh orange juice**. Proceed with the recipe as directed.

For Grapefruit Curd: Replace the lemon zest with **3 grams (1½ teaspoons) grapefruit zest** and the lemon juice with **95 grams (6 tablespoons) strained fresh grapefruit juice.** Proceed with the recipe as directed.

MY GO-TO DARK CHOCOLATE GANACHE

Don't be intimidated by the fancy name—chocolate ganache is just a mixture of chocolate and cream. A good chocolate ganache recipe is incredibly versatile. It can be infused with herbs and spices to create vibrant and flavorful fillings for truffles, or even melted into milk to make a rich cup of cocoa. When liquid, ganache can be used to glaze a cake; when set, it can be whipped and used to fill or even frost cakes.

MAKES: 500 grams (2 cups), enough to fill one 8-inch tart or one two-layered 8-inch or 20 cm cake, with leftover ganache
TIME: 15 minutes

INGREDIENTS

220 grams	¾ cup + 3 tablespoons	heavy cream
45 grams	3 tablespoons	whole milk
220 grams	7¼ ounces	semisweet or bittersweet dark chocolate,* chopped (about 1¼ cups)
45 grams	1½ tablespoons	unsalted butter, at room temperature

* *It's important to use a good-quality dark chocolate like Valrhona. Some chocolate bars contain additives or artificial ingredients that will prevent you from getting the silky consistency you're aiming for when making ganache.*

1. **Make the cream mixture:** Combine the cream and the milk in a small saucepan and bring to a boil over medium heat. Remove from the heat.

2. **Combine the cream mixture and the chocolate:** Place the chocolate in a large bowl. Slowly pour the hot cream mixture over the chocolate and whisk until the chocolate has melted and the mixture is smooth.*

   * *You're whisking to melt the chocolate here, not to incorporate air, so stop whisking when all the chocolate has melted.*

3. **Finish the ganache:** Add the butter and whisk until fully incorporated. Let cool completely.*

   * *Adding butter softens the ganache and makes it smoother.*

STORAGE

The ganache can be stored in the refrigerator in an airtight container, with plastic wrap pressed directly against the surface of the ganache, for up to 3 days.

BEST FOR

> Filling tarts and light cakes—this is a rich filling, so I usually recommend a thin slice of chocolate ganache tart.

> Glazing (i.e., finishing) mousse cakes—just keep in mind that unlike My Go-To Dark Chocolate Glaze (page 230), ganache is matte and not shiny when set

> Truffles (below)—ganache rolled and finished with unsweetened cocoa powder

TRUFFLES

If you have extra ganache, cover the bowl and refrigerate the ganache for at least 2 hours, or until set. Scoop a tablespoon of the chilled ganache and roll it into a ball with your hands, then place it on a parchment paper–lined sheet pan; repeat with the remaining ganache. Scoop 65 grams (½ cup) unsweetened cocoa powder into a large bowl. Drop in a few balls of ganache at a time and toss to coat. Store the truffles in an airtight container in the refrigerator for up to 3 days.

BASIL TRUFFLES
FILLING: Basil Dark Chocolate Ganache (page 142)
FINISHING: Cocoa powder
TECHNIQUE: Truffles (page 140)

SPICE- OR HERB-INFUSED DARK CHOCOLATE GANACHE

Fresh herbs and spices add a subtle hint of flavor to chocolate ganache without compromising its smooth and silky texture. The trick is to infuse the cream with the herb or spice before using it in the ganache, which imparts the flavor of the ingredient into the cream but does not change its texture. When cooking and baking with herbs, a little bit goes a long way—and dried herbs are more potent than fresh. You can always add more, but it's much harder to take away, so start with a small amount. You can steep your cream mixture longer if you're craving a stronger flavor. Think of it like making tea: you add an ingredient to the warm cream mixture, steep, and voilà. Here are three variations to try: basil, lavender, and star anise.

ADDED EQUIPMENT
Fine-mesh sieve

THE CHANGE

In step 1 of **My Go-To Dark Chocolate Ganache** (page 137), after removing the cream mixture from the heat, whisk in **7 grams (16 or 17) fresh basil leaves,*** **1 gram (1 tablespoon) culinary-grade lavender, or 3 grams (1½ pods) star anise**.* Cover the pan with a lid or plastic wrap and let stand for 15 minutes to infuse. Strain the cream mixture through a fine-mesh sieve; discard the solids. Proceed with the recipe as directed.

* * *To maximize the flavor of the basil, pound the leaves with the back of a knife to release their essential oils.*

* * *Star anise pods are easy to break into smaller pieces with your hands.*

FRUIT PURÉE CHOCOLATE GANACHE

Fresh fruit purées can add sweetness, and sometimes tang, to dark chocolate ganache. Choose fruits that are bright in flavor and go well with chocolate, like raspberry, strawberry, cherry, or banana.

MAKES: 700 grams (2¾ cups), enough to fill one 8-inch tart or one two-layered 8-inch or 20 cm cake, with leftover ganache

THE CHANGE

In step 2 of **My Go-To Dark Chocolate Ganache** (page 137), add **200 grams (¾ cup) room-temperature raspberry, strawberry, cherry, or banana purée*** to the bowl with the chocolate before adding the hot cream mixture. Proceed with the recipe as directed. The additional liquid from the fruit purée will make this ganache a bit looser, but it can be used in the same way as my go-to ganache for frosting and glazing cakes (page 178).

> * *Prepared fruit purées can be found in specialty stores and online. To make your own, in a blender, purée 200 grams (about 1½ cups) fresh or frozen fruit until smooth. If the fruit has seeds, like strawberries and raspberries, strain the purée through a fine-mesh sieve to remove them.*

COCONUT MILK DARK CHOCOLATE GANACHE

FILLING

MY GO-TO DARK
CHOCOLATE GANACHE

Replacing the milk and cream in my dark chocolate ganache with coconut milk makes this a dairy-free alternative. To keep this recipe dairy-free, be sure to use dark chocolate, not milk chocolate or white chocolate.

THE CHANGE

Prepare **My Go-To Dark Chocolate Ganache** (page 137) as directed, but replace the heavy cream and milk with **260 grams (1 cup) full-fat coconut milk** and omit the butter in step 3. The consistency of this ganache will be slightly softer when set, but it can be used in the same way as my go-to ganache for frosting and glazing cakes (page 178).

SPIKED DARK CHOCOLATE GANACHE

FILLING

MY GO-TO DARK
CHOCOLATE GANACHE

Nothing pairs better with chocolate than alcohol. The flavor of chocolate is strong, and it needs a potent-flavored liquor—like bourbon, port, or Kahlúa—to balance it.

THE CHANGE

Prepare **My Go-To Dark Chocolate Ganache** (page 137) as directed. While the ganache is still warm, pour in **15 grams (1 tablespoon) bourbon, port, or Kahlúa** and whisk until combined. Let cool completely.

Never Throw Away Leftovers

Growing up with few resources left my family scrambling to put food on the table. We were a household of six—my parents, my three siblings, and my grandmother, plus all our cats and dogs—living solely off my dad's factory-worker salary. In France, salaries were paid out on a monthly basis, and without proper budgeting, we'd often be out of money for food toward the end of the month. The thing is, when you have only a little, you learn to do a lot with it.

This was especially true of food. It was mesmerizing to watch my mom pull together dinner each night. On the first night, she would slow roast a whole chicken over diced root vegetables. The next night, she would pick off whatever meat was left on the chicken carcass and toss it with pasta, adding the leftover roasted potatoes and carrots from the night before. Finally, on night three, she would stew the chicken bones and any leftover vegetables in water, then blend it all together to create a flavorful broth. My mom was not a great cook, but I still loved watching her and offering my hand. How magical it was that we could resurrect a handful of humble ingredients each night, allowing them to live out three lives instead of one. It was during these moments that I first understood what it means to truly know how to cook. To cook is to love each component or ingredient for its entire lifetime.

We didn't eat dessert often. Once in a while, for a special occasions, there would be something sweet—a simple vanilla cake with pastry cream, Chantilly cream, and fresh strawberries from the supermarket. No matter how full I was, I would always clear my plate for that rare piece of cake. But leftover cake was nowhere near as magical as leftover chicken. You couldn't repurpose it into something else entirely, so we would send the remaining slices home with our guests, or eat them ourselves until the cake was too stale to enjoy. The life of a cake felt disappointingly short. And for years, I mistakenly thought I couldn't be creative when it came to leftover desserts.

On my first day of culinary school, I realized the opposite was true. Opening up the pastry walk-in freezer, I realized that almost nothing was ever thrown away. Each ingredient was wrapped tightly, labeled with the date and ingredient name with a Sharpie on kitchen masking tape, and stacked on sheet trays. All the purées were on one side, finished items and ice cream on the other side, and the prep in the middle. There was a stash of doughs and creams lying dormant, waiting to transform into a dessert. Cake scraps, left over from trimming sheets of chocolate cake for chocolate mousse entrêmets, were not thrown away; they were toasted and crumbled over ice cream. Ganache could be frozen and rolled into truffles.

Some might have seen these rows of labeled components as leftovers, but not the way I did. I felt the same wealth of possibilities that I did when I watched my mother roast a whole chicken. I was raised not to see lack, but potential. In between lectures and demonstrations, imagining the possibilities of each building block in the pastry walk-in freezer became one of my favorite activities. And that's what I want to teach you about cooking and baking: each recipe is never just for one dessert, but the component for an infinite variety of desserts.

At the end of a long day of classes, we'd always clean up the kitchen and classroom together. I noticed how flimsy the trash cans were, with just a ring on top to hold the bag and a base. Each trash bag was thin and transparent, and I wondered why we didn't go for more durable options. Then one day, I saw the chef looking intently at a trash bag. I watched as he opened it and started to dig into it, removing its contents. A student had tossed away some bruised berries that were not suitable for a tart. Furious, the chef picked out the berries one by one and made the student wash and dry them. The bruised berries were eventually turned into perfectly delicious jam, and everyone realized the purpose of the clear trash bags. I laughed as I realized I was just where I had started: making treasure out of trash—and, most important, knowing that the "trash" was always a treasure to begin with.

MY GO-TO
APPLE COMPOTE

Folding fresh fruit into a cake batter can sometimes result in a soggy mess once baked. Compotes, in which fruits are cooked down until thickened but still have chunks of fruit in tact, are my secret ingredient in many cakes and tarts. They add both the texture and flavor of fresh fruit—without the excess moisture. If you prefer chunky peanut butter over smooth, choose compotes over jams or gelées when you bake.

MAKES: 300 grams (1¼ cups), enough to fill one 8-inch tart or one two-layered 8-inch or 20 cm cake, with leftover compote
TIME: 1 hour 30 minutes

INGREDIENTS

525 grams	6	Honeycrisp apples, peeled, cored, and cut into ½-inch (1.5 cm) cubes*
50 grams	¼ cup	granulated sugar
25 grams	1 tablespoon + 2 teaspoons	water
6 grams	1	Tahitian vanilla bean, split lengthwise, seeds scraped

* *In place of the Honeycrisps, you can use Gala apples.*

Combine the apples, sugar, water, and vanilla seeds in a large saucepan and bring to a simmer over medium heat. Cook, stirring occasionally, until all the liquid has evaporated and the compote has thickened, 30 to 45 minutes. The apples should be golden brown and soft but still chunky. Cover and let cool completely.

STORAGE

The compote can be stored in an airtight container in the refrigerator for up to 3 days.

BEST FOR

> Fruit tarts, caramelized fruit tarts (on sablé Breton is my favorite), or lighter cakes

PEAR COMPOTE

Pear is a subtle flavor compared to many fruits, but it works well with different spices from cinnamon to sage to peppercorns, so it makes for a versatile fruit that can be pulled into many different directions.

MAKES: 300 grams (1¼ cups), enough to fill one 8-inch tart or one two-layered 8-inch or 20 cm cake, with leftover compote
TIME: 1 hour

THE CHANGE

Prepare **My Go-To Apple Compote** (page 150) as directed, replacing the apples with **525 grams (7) Bosc, Bartlett, or Anjou pears,** peeled, cored, and cut into ½-inch (1.5 cm) cubes.

MANGO COMPOTE

FILLING

MY GO-TO APPLE COMPOTE

There's nothing like juicy in-season mangoes—and you can preserve that flavor by turning ripe mangoes into a compote. I love Alphonso mangoes for their silky, creamy texture, but they can be hard to find. Ataulfo or Champagne mangoes, which are readily available in many markets, work well, too.

MAKES: 300 grams (1¼ cups), enough to fill one 8-inch tart or one two-layered 8-inch or 20 cm cake, with leftover compote
TIME: 1 hour

THE CHANGE

Prepare **My Go-To Apple Compote** (page 150) as directed, but replace the apples with **570 grams (3½ cups) ripe diced peeled mangoes** and the granulated sugar with **28 grams (2¼ tablespoons) brown sugar**. Because the mangoes are tender, not firm, this compote will cook faster, in just 10 to 15 minutes. The mangoes should be soft but still chunky.

RHUBARB COMPOTE

Fresh rhubarb is only in season for a few weeks each spring. Look for stalks that are pink or reddish in color, as they're the most tender—and the most flavorful.

MAKES: 300 grams (1¼ cups), enough to fill one 8-inch tart or one two-layered 8-inch or 20 cm cake, with leftover compote

TIME: 1 hour

INGREDIENTS

4 grams	1⅓ teaspoons	powdered apple pectin*
150 grams	¾ cup	granulated sugar
435 grams	about 1 lb or 4⅓ cups	rhubarb, washed, peeled, and cut into ½-inch (1.5 cm) pieces
6 grams	1	Tahitian vanilla bean, split lengthwise, seeds scraped
		Natural red food coloring (optional)

 * *Rhubarb contains a lot of water. Adding pectin helps thicken the compote.*

THE CHANGE

1. Make the pectin mixture: Combine the pectin and 55 grams (¼ cup) of the sugar in a small bowl and stir with a spoon until well mixed.

2. Make the compote: Combine the rhubarb, remaining 110 grams (½ cup) sugar, and vanilla seeds in a large saucepan and bring to a boil over medium heat. Add the pectin mixture* and stir until incorporated. Reduce the heat to low, cover, and simmer until all the liquid has evaporated and the compote has thickened, 30 to 45 minutes. The rhubarb should be soft but still chunky.

 * *It's important to wait until the compote mixture is boiling before adding the pectin mixture, or the pectin will clump.*

3. Tint the compote, if desired: If you'd like to heighten the compote's pink color, add a few drops of red food coloring, stirring after each drop before adding another—use it sparingly and stop when you've reached the desired shade of pink.

4. Let cool: Cover the compote and let cool completely.

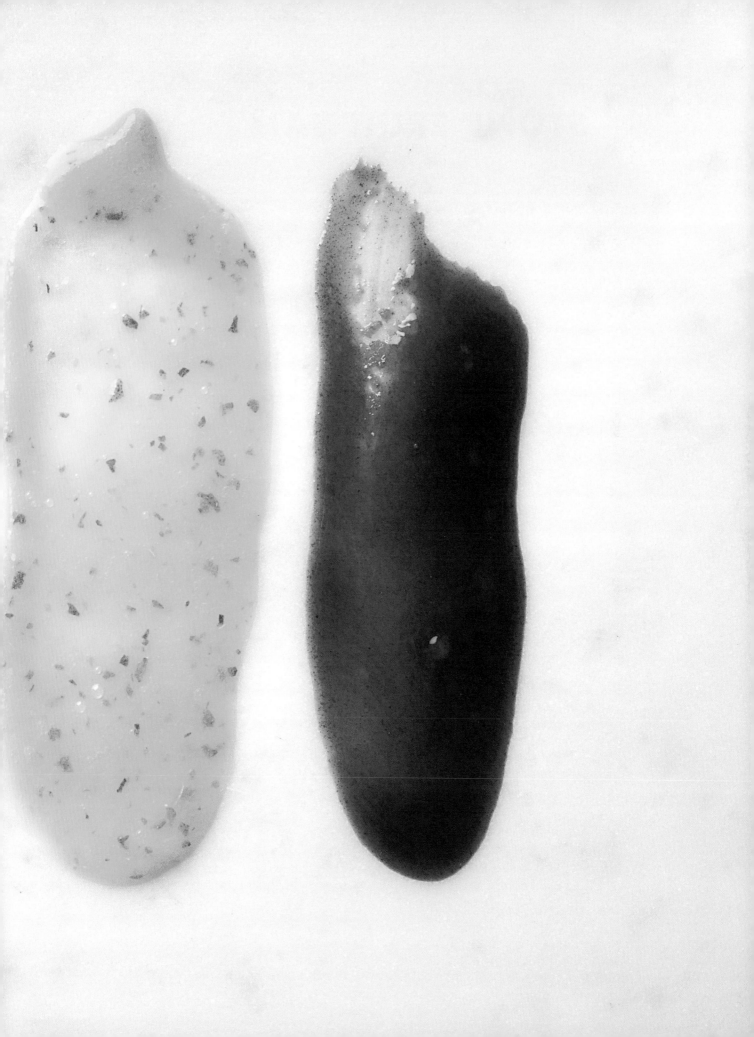

MY GO-TO STONE FRUIT JAM

Think of jam as a way to make fruit taste instantly riper: this process intensifies flavor and preserves it. That's why they are such great additions to cakes and tarts, both in and out of season. I often fill raspberries tarts with raspberry jam to amplify them, so pockets of jam burst out when you take a bite. And of course, extra jam never goes to waste—spread it over toast or swirl it into vanilla ice cream.

MAKES: 600 grams (2½ cups), enough to fill one 8-inch tart or one two-layered 8-inch or 20 cm cake, with leftover jam

TIME: about 1 hour

INGREDIENTS

200 grams	1 cup	granulated sugar
24 grams	2 tablespoons + 1¾ teaspoons	powdered apple pectin
700 grams	8	fresh large peaches, peeled,* pitted, and cut into cubes
30 grams	2 tablespoons	fresh lemon juice
20 grams	4 teaspoons	rum

* *Here's an easy way to peel peaches: Bring a large pot of water to a boil. Fill a large bowl with ice and water and set it nearby. Score an "x" at the bottom of each peach with a paring knife, then add them to the boiling water and blanch for about 45 seconds. Drain the peaches, then plunge them into the ice water to stop them from cooking further. Drain, then use your hands to easily remove the skin from each peach.*

1. Make the pectin mixture: Combine the sugar and pectin in a medium bowl and stir until well mixed.

2. Make the peach mixture: Combine the peaches, lemon juice, and rum in a large bowl. Sprinkle the pectin mixture evenly over the peaches* and stir until incorporated.

    * *Make sure to sprinkle the pectin mixture evenly, or it will clump.*

3. Cook the jam: Transfer the peach mixture to a medium saucepan, cover, and bring to a simmer over medium heat. Cook, stirring occasionally and adjusting the heat as needed if the mixture threatens to boil over, until the peaches have broken down and the mixture is thick and jammy, 30 to 45 minutes. Remove from the heat.

4. Use or store the jam: If you'll be using the jam immediately or within a few days, let it cool completely; otherwise, process the jam for long-term storage while it's still hot (page 158).

STORAGE

The jam is best enjoyed the same day it's made, but once cooled, it can be stored in an airtight container in the refrigerator for up to 4 days.

BEST FOR

> Jams are very versatile and can be used between cake layers or in tarts, or even sandwiched between cookies

CANNING JAM FOR LONG-TERM STORAGE

If you'd like to store your jam for longer than a few days, follow these steps to safely process it.

1. Sterilize the jars: Fit a wire rack inside a deep pot. Place your jam jars (right-side up), lids,* and rings on the rack. Fill the pot with enough water to completely submerge the jars and bring the water to a boil. Boil for 10 minutes, then turn off the heat, leaving the jars and lids in the hot water.

> * *Some lids are not heatproof and cannot be boiled. If your lids have plastic or rubber linings, put them in a separate large saucepan, add water to cover them completely, and bring the water to a simmer (do not boil!). Simmer for 10 minutes.*

2. Dry the jars: Spread a clean kitchen towel over a work surface. Using tongs, remove the jars from the water and place them upside down on the towel to dry. Transfer the lids to the towel to dry as well. Let the jars and lids stand until completely dry. Drain the water from the pot (leave the rack inside).

3. Fill the jars: While the jars are still hot, turn them right-side up and fill each with jam, leaving about half an inch of headspace. Wipe the rims clean. Seal tightly with the lids.

4. Boil the jars: Place the filled jars on the rack in the pot. Add water to fully submerge the jars and bring the water to a boil. Boil for 5 minutes.

5. Seal the jars: Remove the jars from the water using tongs. The jars will seal as they cool down. To test that the jar has properly sealed, press down on the center of the lid. It should not spring up or down. You can also tell if the jam is sealed well by hearing a pop sound. You can also hold up the jar and look at the lid to see that it is slightly concaving in to indicate a vacuum is formed inside keeping things airtight.

STORE THE JAM

Store the sealed jars of jam at room temperature for up to 3 months. Once opened, store the jam in the refrigerator for up to 1 week.

BERRY JAM

I love making jam with ripe fresh berries to preserve the very best of summer. Use your favorite berries—strawberries, blueberries, raspberries, blackberries, or huckleberries all work well here.

THE CHANGE

Prepare **My Go-To Stone Fruit Jam** (page 156) as directed, but replace the peaches with **700 grams (4½ cups) ripe fresh berries*** and omit the rum and lemon juice.

* *If you prefer your jam to be seedless—if you're making a blackberry jam, for example—strain it through a fine-mesh sieve before letting it cool.*

RASPBERRY CREAM PUFF CAKE
BASE: Round Choux Base, with Profiterole Top (page 112)
FILLING: Raspberry Jam (page 159)
FINISHING: Fresh raspberries (page 248) + Vanilla Chantilly Cream (page 252)

FIG JAM

FILLING

MY GO-TO STONE FRUIT JAM

Figs are one of my favorite fruits, and when they're in season during the summer, I'll eat them any way I can—especially fresh or made into this fig jam.

THE CHANGE

In step 1 of **My Go-To Stone Fruit Jam** (page 156), use **250 grams (1¼ cups) granulated sugar and 15 grams (1 tablespoon plus 2 teaspoons) powdered apple pectin**. In step 2, replace the peaches with **730 grams (3¼ cups) fresh figs,*** chopped. Proceed with the recipe as directed. The figs will break down faster than the peaches, so the mixture should be thick and jammy in just 10 to 15 minutes.

*   *I like black Mission figs, but Turkish brown figs also work.*

CHERRY JAM

Adding a splash of kirsch, a cherry brandy, helps to balance the flavors and sweetness of this cherry jam.

INGREDIENTS

30 grams	2 tablespoons + 1¼ teaspoons	granulated sugar
8 grams	2½ teaspoons	powdered apple pectin
700 grams	3 cups	fresh cherries,* stemmed, pitted, and chopped
300 grams	1½ cups	granulated sugar
17 grams	4 teaspoons	kirsch

    * *Bing and Rainier cherries are my favorites. Make sure the cherries are firm, not mushy.*

THE CHANGE

1. Make the pectin mixture: Combine 30 grams (2 tablespoons plus 1¼ teaspoons) of the sugar and the pectin in a small bowl and stir until well mixed.

2. Make the cherry mixture: Combine the cherries and remaining 320 grams (1½ cups) sugar in a large bowl. Sprinkle the pectin mixture evenly over the cherries* and stir until incorporated.

    * *Make sure to sprinkle the pectin mixture evenly, or it will clump.*

3. Cook the jam: Transfer the cherry mixture to a medium saucepan, cover, and bring to a simmer over medium heat. Cook, stirring occasionally and adjusting the heat as needed if the mixture threatens to boil over, until the cherries have broken down and the mixture is thick, 15 to 20 minutes. Remove from the heat.

4. Finish the jam: Add the kirsch and stir with a spatula to combine.

CHOCOLATE CHERRY CAKE
BASE: Brownie Base (page 84)
FILLING: Cherry Jam (page 163)
FINISHING: Chocolate Buttercream (page 222) + Fresh cherries (page 248)
TECHNIQUE: How to Assemble a Layer Cake (page 293)

CHERRY TART
BASE: Vanilla Sablé Tart Shell (page 4)
FILLING: Pastry Cream (page 121) + Cherry Jam (page 163) + Almond Cake (page 34)
FINISHING: Nappage Glaze (page 223) + Fresh cherries (page 248)
TECHNIQUE: How to Build a Tart (page 286)

MY GO-TO FRUIT GELÉE

A gelée is a fruit-based jelly set in a disc. It's smoother and less sweet than both compote and jam. When used as a filling in a layer cake, a gelée adds both height and flavor. The disc is a perfect, even thickness, and works well as a layer in mousse cakes.

The texture of a finished gelée depends on the type of gelling agent used to make it. In baking, we typically rely on two gelling agents, which we use for different purposes:

> Gelatin, an animal-based product, is used to create a set gelée to build layers in cakes.

> Pectin, which is extracted from the seeds of fruits, is used to create a thicker, jam-like gelée that's more spreadable.

This recipe uses powdered gelatin, which is the most common and readily available type.

MAKES: One 8-inch (20 cm) disc (¼ inch or 6 mm thick)
TIME: 30 to 40 minutes (not including resting overnight)

INGREDIENTS

20 grams	4 teaspoons	cold water
4 grams	1⅓ teaspoons	unflavored powdered gelatin
185 grams	¾ cup + 1½ teaspoons	raspberry, blueberry, or apricot purée*
30 grams	2½ tablespoons	granulated sugar

* Prepared raspberry, blueberry, and apricot purées can be found in specialty stores and online. To make your own, in a blender, purée 185 grams (1½ cups) fresh raspberries or blueberries or 250 grams (2 cups) peeled and pitted apricots until smooth, then strain (if you prefer the seeds of the raspberries or blueberries, you do not need to strain).

EQUIPMENT

8-inch (20 cm) round silicone mold or cake ring
Silicone baking mat (optional, if using a cake ring)

1. Dissolve the gelatin: Combine the cold water and gelatin in a small bowl and stir with a spoon until the gelatin has dissolved.

2. Cook the gelée: In a medium saucepan, bring the raspberry purée to a simmer over medium heat, whisking occasionally. Add the sugar and the gelatin mixture and whisk to combine. Bring to a boil over medium heat,* whisking constantly to make sure there are no lumps, and cook for 2 minutes. Remove from the heat.

> * *You won't see any visual changes in the consistency; boiling just melts the gelatin.*

3. Set the gelée: Pour the gelée into an 8-inch (20 cm) round silicone mold. (Alternatively, line a sheet pan with a silicone baking mat, set an 8-inch (20 cm) cake ring on the mat, and pour the gelée into the cake ring.) Freeze the gelée until firm, at least 5 hours or overnight. To unmold, gently lift the cake ring while pressing down on the edges of the gelée.

STORAGE

The disc of gelée can be wrapped tightly in plastic wrap and stored in the freezer for up to 5 days. You can assemble the cake straight from the frozen gelée, but it needs to temper in the refrigerator prior to serving.

BEST FOR

> Mousse cakes

PASSION FRUIT GELÉE

I love the flavor of passion fruit—it's sharp, floral, and fruity, and pairs with anything from chocolate to matcha to coffee. Passion fruit is more acidic than raspberries or blueberries, so it will require more gelatin to set.

THE CHANGE

Prepare **My Go-To Fruit Gelée** (page 168) as directed, but use **30 grams (2 tablespoons) cold water and 6 grams (2 teaspoons) unflavored powdered gelatin** and replace the raspberry or blueberry purée with **185 grams (¾ cup + 1½ teaspoons) passion fruit purée or juice**.

SPREADABLE PEACH GELÉE (WITH PECTIN)

This variation creates a spreadable fruit gelée. It follows the same general method as in My Go-To Fruit Gelée (page 168), with a few tweaks. Pectin doesn't need to be bloomed in water as gelatin does, but it does need to be cooked a bit longer to help the gelée set correctly.

MAKES: 290 grams (1 cup) enough to fill one 8-inch tart or one two-layered 8-inch or 20 cm cake, with leftover gelée
TIME: 30 to 40 minutes (not including resting overnight)

INGREDIENTS

195 grams	¾ cup + 1¼ tablespoons	peach purée*
100 grams	½ cup	granulated sugar
5 grams	1⅓ teaspoons	powdered pectin*

* *Prepared peach purée can be found in specialty stores and online. To make your own, in a blender, purée 195 grams (about 1 cup) pitted peeled fresh peaches until smooth (see page 156 for a tip on peeling peaches).*

* *Gelée made with pectin does not set as firmly as gelée made with gelatin. When ready to use, keep this gelée cold, work quickly, and use a bench scraper to help place it on your cake.*

THE CHANGE

1. Cook the gelée: Put the peach purée in a medium saucepan and bring to a simmer over medium heat, whisking occasionally. Add the sugar and the pectin and whisk to combine. Bring to a boil, whisking constantly to avoid lumps, and cook for 3 minutes, until the bubbles slow and the mixture thickens. Remove from the heat.

2. Set the gelée: Pour the gelée into an 8-inch (20 cm) round silicone mold or cake ring set over a silicone mat. Freeze until firm, at least 5 hours or overnight.

To Learn How to Cook,
First Learn How to Taste

Growing up, one of my favorite movies was *L'aile ou la cuisse* (*The Wing or the Leg*). The title refers to your choice when it comes to roast chicken: drumstick or wing? In the film, Louis de Funès, a French actor prominent in the 1960s and '70s, plays a restaurant critic who always goes above and beyond for his job. Louis dons elaborate disguises—facial prosthetics, wigs, costumes—when he goes to review a restaurant. He tucks tweezers in the hidden pockets of his jacket and uses them to steal samples of the food for laboratory testing later. As he goes through this ritual, the audience waits in suspense. Each raise of an eyebrow is a sign of Louis's opinion; a curl of the lip, in either direction, is his decree.

In one scene, the restaurant is tipped off: they know Louis will be coming in that day, so the staff rushes to prepare. Is the glassware polished? Is the linen pressed? The maître d' surveils the dining room like a hawk, watching each diner for signs of a secret identity. Sadly, the staff is fooled by Louis's disguise (this time, he arrives dressed as an elderly woman). Louis watches as plate after plate of complimentary food is sent to an unassuming single diner misidentified as the toughest critic in town. In the meantime, he has a hard time even waving down one of the panicked servers.

The more the waiters fumbled in Louis's presence, the more I laughed. I'd point to the television screen as they sweated. I didn't know then that one day I would become a chef and find it harder to laugh at the same scenes after having often been on the other side, sweating myself.

L'aile ou la cuisse made it clear that the critic had the upper hand over the cook. A critic represents the voice of the guests, and what good is a chef's food if it isn't enjoyed by those guests? These days, when we get a tip that a critic is in the house, we certainly make the rounds and triple check to make sure everything is at its best. But our service is never focused solely on one person. Every guest sitting in the dining room is a critic whose opinion we value.

Over the years, I've received good reviews and bad reviews. My reaction to these reviews has also varied. I've felt grateful to a critic for pointing out something that I missed. I've fumed over a review without any real content. And I've given many reviews to my team, too. Too salty, too sweet, not enough flavor, not enough finesse—criticisms are almost always in the eye (or on the tongue) of the beholder. I know many chefs who have simply

given up reacting to criticism. "You can't please everyone," they say. But I happen to believe differently. I take almost all feedback into consideration, whether or not I agree with it. Sometimes it's about seasoning—with our shops around the world, what is sweet to one location isn't for another. Other times it's about execution—something overcooked or undercooked. And many times it's not about the food at all, but the service. Each comment launches a small investigation into what happened and how we can make it better. To me, critiques are never a permanent judgment, but a progressive suggestion for improvement.

As a kid, I was entertained by the slapstick comedy in *L'aile ou la cuisse*, but I was more intrigued by the details of running a restaurant. Louis opened up my mind to the exotic culinary world. As Louis prepares his reviews, he looks at the music, the service, the wine—he can tell the varietal just by swirling his glass and taking a quick taste. From French fine dining to Japanese teppanyaki, his expertise amazed me. What a life! First, to feast. And then, to talk to the world about each detail, from the type of plate the dish was served on to the candle in the center of the table.

But here's the biggest lesson I've learned: in order to learn how to cook, you first need to learn how to taste, and you must keep accessing your palate as the times change. Just as you practice how to cook, you must eat many things to learn how to taste. My own palate has changed considerably as I've moved around the world and exposed it to new flavors. I delighted in the spice of chiles when I traveled around Southeast Asia, and I learned to appreciate the bitterness in my first sip of amaro in Italy. You've already experienced something comparable just by growing up—those vegetables you couldn't stand as a child might now be some of your favorite ingredients. The sour and burning flavor of wine that you couldn't stand the first time you tried it is now a delight for your more mature palate. It's important to learn not just how to sharpen your knives and measure out your ingredients, but how to taste foods and push your tastes forward. Recipes are templates, forever open to alterations as tastes grow and change.

I recently watched *L'aile ou la cuisse* again, and Louis was just as I had remembered him. In one scene, he takes a bite of a perfectly cooked steak and sighs in enjoyment. Delighted, he wipes his mouth with a napkin and shouts, "Bravo!" That's when I realized that neither Louis nor the chef had the upper hand. They were comrades. In real life, it is also never a battle between critic and chef. The very best chefs are always both.

MY GO-TO MASCARPONE WHIPPED GANACHE

Whipped ganache is the one filling I use the most. Think of it as very stable whipped cream—adding a bit of gelatin keeps it from deflating or leaking over time. This mascarpone whipped ganache is delicious with all sorts of fruit; I love it best with cherries and dark chocolate.

MAKES: 1 kilogram (4 cups), enough to fill two 8-inch tarts or one three-layered 8-inch or 20 cm cake, with leftover ganache

TIME: 30 minutes, plus resting overnight

INGREDIENTS

8 grams	2½ teaspoons	unflavored powdered gelatin
40 grams	2 tablespoons + 1¾ teaspoons	cold water
415 grams	1¾ cups	heavy cream
380 grams	1½ cups	mascarpone cheese
50 grams	2¼ tablespoons	honey
155 grams	5½ ounces	white chocolate, finely chopped

EQUIPMENT

Stand mixer with whisk attachment or hand mixer

1. **Dissolve the gelatin:** Combine the gelatin and cold water in a small bowl and stir with a spoon until the gelatin has dissolved.

2. **Make the hot cream mixture:** Combine the cream, mascarpone, and honey in a medium saucepan and bring to a boil over medium heat. Remove from the heat and whisk in the gelatin mixture until incorporated.

3. **Make the ganache:** Place the white chocolate in a large heatproof bowl. Without stirring, slowly pour the hot cream mixture over the chocolate. Let stand for 30 seconds, then whisk until the chocolate has melted and the mixture is smooth. Cover with plastic wrap pressed directly against the surface of the ganache to prevent a skin from forming. Refrigerate overnight. (At this point, the unwhipped ganache can be stored for later use—see Storage.)

4. Whip the ganache: When you're ready to fill your tart or frost your cake, transfer the chilled ganache to the bowl of a stand mixer fitted with the whisk attachment and immediately* whip on high speed until light and fluffy, about 4 to 5 minutes. (Alternatively, leave it in the large bowl and whip with a hand mixer.)* Use immediately.

* *Make sure that the ganache is cold. If it's at room temperature, it won't whip up.*

* *When frosting a cake with whipped ganache, be careful not to run your spatula over the ganache too many times, or you'll overwork the cream and it'll become grainy.*

STORAGE

Whipped ganache is best used right away. Unwhipped ganache can be stored in the refrigerator in an airtight container, with plastic wrap pressed against the surface of the ganache, for up to 3 days. Whip just before using.

BEST FOR

> One of the most versatile fillings for tarts, any type of cake, or éclairs
> Topping a pavlova

LYCHEE WHIPPED GANACHE

Once you've mastered My Go-To Whipped Ganache, add fruit purée to mix things up. I love using lychees to add a bright, tropical flavor.

INGREDIENTS

12 grams	3¾ teaspoons + ⅛ teaspoon	unflavored powdered gelatin
60 grams	¼ cup	cold water
575 grams	2½ cups	heavy cream
175 grams	6 ounces	white chocolate, finely chopped
240 grams	¾ cup	lychee purée*

* *Prepared lychee purée can be found in specialty stores and online. To make your own, in a blender, purée 200 grams (about 1½ cups) canned lychees until smooth. Strain the purée through a fine-mesh sieve.*

THE CHANGE

1. Dissolve the gelatin: Combine the gelatin and cold water in a small bowl and stir with a spoon until the gelatin has dissolved.

2. Make the hot cream mixture: Put the cream in a medium saucepan and bring to a boil over medium heat. Remove from the heat and whisk in the gelatin mixture until incorporated.

3. Make the ganache: Place the white chocolate and lychee purée in a large heatproof bowl. Without stirring, slowly pour the hot cream mixture over the chocolate and lychee purée. Let stand for 30 seconds, then whisk until the chocolate has melted and the mixture is smooth. Cover with plastic wrap pressed directly against the surface of the ganache to prevent a skin from forming. Refrigerate overnight.

4. When you're ready to fill or frost your cake, whip the ganache as directed in **My Go-To Mascarpone Whipped Ganache** (page 178).

COCONUT WHIPPED GANACHE

For an especially smooth and creamy whipped ganache, replace the mascarpone in My Go-To Mascarpone Whipped Ganache with coconut milk. (The subtle coconut flavor is a bonus.)

THE CHANGE

Prepare **My Go-To Mascarpone Whipped Ganache** (page 178) as directed, but replace the mascarpone with **350 grams (1½ cups) coconut milk**. Note that when you chill this ganache, it won't fully set.

CHOCOLATE CHIP COOKIE COCONUT CAKE
BASE: Cookie Base (page 76) + Chocolate Cake (page 22)
FILLING: Coconut Whipped Ganache (page 181)
FINISHING: Italian Meringue (page 258)
TECHNIQUE: How to Assemble a Layer Cake (page 293)

CRÈME FRAÎCHE
WHIPPED GANACHE

Swapping in crème fraîche for the mascarpone gives this filling a tangier flavor and lighter texture, which works especially well with a sweet base like My Go-To Cookie Base (page 76) or My Go-To Chocolate Brownies (page 84).

THE CHANGE

Prepare **My Go-To Mascarpone Whipped Ganache** (page 178) as directed, but replace the mascarpone with **380 grams (1½ cups) crème fraîche**.

STRAWBERRY HONEY CRÈME FRAÎCHE TART
BASE: Vanilla Sablé Tart Shell (page 4)

FILLING: Pastry Cream (page 121) + Crème Fraîche

Whipped Ganache (page 184) + Strawberry Jam (page 159)

FINISHING: Fresh strawberries (page 248), honeycomb, Nappage Glaze (page 223)

TECHNIQUE: How to Build a Tart (page 286)

MUSCOVADO SUGAR WHIPPED GANACHE

I love the rich, molasses-like flavor of muscovado sugar. Here we're turning My Go-To Mascarpone Whipped Ganache recipe into a muscovado version by simply replacing the honey with muscovado sugar.

THE CHANGE

In step 2 of **My Go-To Mascarpone Whipped Ganache** (page 178), omit the mascarpone and use **740 grams (3 cups + 2 tablespoons) heavy cream**, and replace the honey with **90 grams (½ cup) muscovado sugar**.* Proceed with the recipe as directed.

> * If you can't find muscovado sugar, dark brown sugar is a perfect substitute.

VANILLA WHIPPED GANACHE

Perhaps the most versatile ganache of all, vanilla whipped ganache pairs well with everything from bright fruits to floral and aromatic herbs to decadent chocolate and caramel.

INGREDIENTS

9 grams	1 tablespoon	unflavored powdered gelatin
45 grams	3 tablespoons	cold water
815 grams	3½ cups	heavy cream
6 grams	1	Tahitian vanilla bean, split lengthwise, seeds scraped
180 grams	6⅓ ounces	white chocolate, finely chopped (about 1 cup)

THE CHANGE

1. Dissolve the gelatin: Combine the gelatin and cold water in a small bowl and stir with a spoon until the gelatin has dissolved.

2. Make the hot cream mixture: Combine the cream and vanilla seeds in a medium saucepan and bring to a boil over medium heat. Remove from the heat and whisk in the gelatin mixture until incorporated.

3. Make the ganache: Place the white chocolate in a large heatproof bowl. Without stirring, slowly pour the hot cream mixture over the chocolate. Let stand for 30 seconds, then whisk until the chocolate has melted and the mixture is smooth. Cover with plastic wrap pressed directly against the surface of the ganache to prevent a skin from forming. Refrigerate overnight.

4. When you're ready to fill or frost your cake, whip the ganache as directed in **My Go-To Mascarpone Whipped Ganache** (page 178).

MY GO-TO
VANILLA MOUSSE

When it comes to mousse cake, the filling is the main event—there's often more filling than base. But mousses are so light and airy, I could eat them by the cupful, with cake or without.

Once you finish making the mousse, you'll need to use it right away to keep that light and airy texture, so make sure you have all your other elements finished and ready to assemble before you start making this filling.

MAKES: 1 kilogram (4 cups), enough for an 8-inch or 20 cm mousse cake, with leftover mousse
TIME: 30 minutes plus chilling time

INGREDIENTS

13 grams	1 tablespoon + ¼ teaspoon	unflavored powdered gelatin
23 grams	4 teaspoons	cold water
405 grams	1⅔ cups	whole milk
6 grams	1	Tahition vanilla bean, split lengthwise, seeds scraped
130 grams	7 large	egg yolks
50 grams	¼ cup	granulated sugar
405 grams	1¾ cups	cold heavy cream

EQUIPMENT
Stand mixer with whisk attachment or hand mixer (optional)

1. Dissolve the gelatin: Combine the gelatin and cold water in a small bowl and stir with a spoon until the gelatin has dissolved.

2. Make the hot milk mixture: Combine the milk and vanilla seeds in a medium saucepan and bring to a boil over medium heat. Remove from the heat and whisk in the gelatin mixture.

3. Make the custard: Whisk together the egg yolks and sugar in a large bowl until combined. While whisking, slowly pour in a little bit of the hot milk mixture to temper the eggs and whisk until combined. Whisk in a bit more of the milk mixture, then pour the tempered egg mixture into the saucepan with the remaining milk mixture.

4. Cook the custard*: Cook the custard over medium-low heat, gently stirring with a spatula, until thick enough to coat the back of the spatula, about 10 minutes. Remove from the heat. Let cool to room temperature, about 30 minutes, or refrigerate for 10 to 15 minutes.

> ✳ *The custard is cooked sufficiently when it has reached a stage called à la nappe, which means it's thick enough to coat the back of a spoon, and when you swipe your finger through it, the line left by your finger remains.*

5. Whip the cream*: In a stand mixer fitted with the whisk attachment (or in a large bowl using a hand mixer or whisk), whip the cream on medium speed until it holds soft peaks, about 5 minutes.

> ✳ *Make sure the cream is cold—room-temperature cream won't whip up as easily.*

6. Finish the mousse: Slowly pour the custard into the whipped cream a little at a time, gently folding with a spatula until just combined. **If you're making a mousse cake**, use the mousse immediately. **If you're making a layer cake**, refrigerate the mousse covered with plastic wrap pressed directly against the surface, until spreadable, about 5 minutes.

STORAGE

If you're using the mousse as a filling to build a cake, you will need to use it right away as it sets. If you are enjoying the mousse on its own, once set, it can be refrigerated with plastic wrap pressed directly against the surface to prevent a skin from forming for up to 4 days.

BEST FOR

> Mousse cake
> On its own: I like to pour mousse into small cups or ramekins, chill it for 45 minutes to 1 hour, then top it with whipped cream for an easy dessert

TEA-FLAVORED MOUSSE

FILLING

MY GO-TO VANILLA
MOUSSE

I love using teas in pastry creams and mousses, like this one. Tea mellows the sweetness of these fillings, bringing balance to your desserts. Matcha and Earl Grey are some of my favorite teas to use.

ADDED EQUIPMENT
Fine-mesh sieve (optional, for Earl Grey variation)

THE CHANGE

In step 2 of **My Go-To Vanilla Mousse** (page 190), prepare the milk mixture as directed, then whisk in **24 grams (¼ cup) matcha green tea powder or 16 grams (¼ cup) loose Earl Grey tea leaves**. If using matcha, proceed with the recipe as directed. If using Earl Grey, cover the pan with a lid or plastic wrap and let stand for 10 minutes to infuse, then strain the milk mixture through a fine-mesh sieve and discard the tea leaves. Proceed with the recipe as directed.

PEAR MOUSSE

FILLING
MY GO-TO VANILLA MOUSSE

Incorporating fruit purée is one of the simplest ways to put a twist on a classic mousse. I love using pears, especially in the winter. To heighten the pear flavor, I sometimes add just a dash of Poire Williams, a pear liqueur, to the custard.

THE CHANGE

In step 2 of **My Go-To Vanilla Mousse** (page 190), add **50 grams (⅕ cup) pear purée*** to the milk mixture before bringing it to a simmer. Proceed with the recipe as directed.

* *Prepared pear purée can be found in specialty stores and online. To make your own, in a blender, purée 50 grams (⅓ cup) cored peeled ripe pears (I like Williams or Bosc, since they have a more vibrant flavor) until smooth.*

OLIVE OIL MOUSSE

FILLING
MY GO-TO VANILLA MOUSSE

Use a grassy green extra-virgin olive oil so its flavor really comes through in the finished mousse. Sometimes, as a trick, I add a few drops of pumpkin seed oil to accentuate this mousse's green color.

THE CHANGE

In step 3 of **My Go-To Vanilla Mousse** (page 190), after pouring the tempered egg mixture into the pan with the remaining milk mixture, add **70 grams (⅓ cup) good-quality extra-virgin olive oil** to the custard and whisk to combine. Proceed with the recipe as directed.

CARAMEL MOUSSE

Caramel is an excellent way to add flavor to fillings—especially mousse. The type of caramel used here is known as a "dry" caramel because it starts with a dry pan, with no water added to the sugar. I like to use the dry method when making caramel-flavored mousses and creams because it allows for more control over the caramelization of the sugar—and therefore over the flavor.

ADDED INGREDIENT

100 grams	½ cup	granulated sugar

THE CHANGE

1. Follow steps 1 and 2 of **My Go-To Vanilla Mousse** (page 190) as directed.

2. Make the dry caramel: Place a small saucepan over medium heat. When the pan is hot, sprinkle a thin, even layer of the sugar over the bottom of the pan. As the sugar melts and caramelizes, slowly whisk in the rest of the sugar, one handful at a time, making sure each handful of sugar has reached an amber brown color before adding another handful. Once all the sugar has been added, cook until it has turned golden amber brown, 1 to 2 minutes.* Remove from the heat immediately to keep it from burning.*

> * *The color of the caramel should be dark so its flavor will carry over when diluted with the milk mixture.*

> * *You can move the saucepan on and off the heat to control the temperature and make sure the sugar doesn't burn.*

3. Combine the caramel and the milk mixture: While whisking, slowly add the hot milk mixture to the caramel and whisk to combine. Be careful, as the caramel might bubble and splatter as you add the milk.

4. Proceed with the recipe as directed.

PEANUT BUTTER MOUSSE

Sweet, salty, and highly addicting, peanut butter mousse is one of my favorite variations.

INGREDIENTS

11 grams	1 tablespoon + ½ teaspoon	unflavored powder gelatin
55 grams	¼ cup	cold water
160 grams	⅔ cup	whole milk
100 grams	5 large	egg yolks
100 grams	½ cup	granulated sugar
225 grams	1 cup	creamy peanut butter
400 grams	1⅔ cups	heavy cream

THE CHANGE

1. Dissolve the gelatin: Combine the gelatin and cold water in a small bowl and stir with a spoon until the gelatin has dissolved.

2. Heat the milk: Put the milk in a medium saucepan and bring to a boil over medium heat. Remove from the heat.

3. Make the custard: Whisk together the egg yolks and sugar in a large bowl until combined. While whisking, slowly pour in a little bit of the hot milk to temper the eggs and whisk until combined. Whisk in a bit more of the milk, then pour the tempered egg mixture into the saucepan with the remaining milk.

4. Cook the custard: Cook the custard over medium-low heat, gently stirring with a spatula, until thick enough to coat the back of the spatula, about 10 minutes. Remove from the heat. While the custard is still warm, add the peanut butter,* then the gelatin mixture, and stir until combined. Let cool completely, about 30 minutes, or refrigerate for 10 to 15 minutes.

> * *If your peanut butter is particularly thick, put it in a medium bowl, add a scoop of the custard, and stir with a spatula to loosen it, then add the peanut butter mixture to the saucepan with the remaining custard.*

5. Whip the cream and finish the mousse as directed in **My Go-To Vanilla Mousse** (page 190).

CHOCOLATE MOUSSE
FILLING: Milk Chocolate Mousse (page 204)
FINISHING: Vanilla Chantilly Cream (page 252)

MY GO-TO DARK CHOCOLATE MOUSSE

This is one for the chocolate lovers. It's rich without being heavy, chocolaty without being too sweet.

MAKES: 1 kilogram (4 cups), enough for an 8-inch or 20 cm mousse cake, with leftover mousse
TIME: 30 minutes plus chilling time

INGREDIENTS

10 grams	1 tablespoon + ¼ teaspoon	gelatin powder
14 grams	1 tablespoon	cold water
245 grams	1 cup	whole milk
305 grams	11 ounces	dark chocolate, chopped
450 grams	1¾ cups + 2 tablespoons	cold heavy cream

1. Dissolve the gelatin: Combine the gelatin and cold water in a small bowl and stir with a spoon until the gelatin has dissolved.

2. Make the hot milk mixture: Put the milk in a medium saucepan and bring to a boil over medium heat. Remove from the heat and whisk in the gelatin mixture.

3. Make the ganache: Place the chocolate in a large heatproof bowl. Without stirring, slowly pour the hot milk mixture over the chocolate. Let stand for 30 seconds, then whisk until the chocolate has melted and the mixture is smooth.

4. Whip the cream: In a stand mixer fitted with the whisk attachment (or in a large bowl using a whisk or hand mixer), whip the cream on medium speed until it holds soft peaks, about 5 minutes.*

> * *Make sure the cream is cold—room-temperature cream won't whip up as easily.*

5. Finish the mousse: While the ganache is still warm, slowly pour it into the whipped cream a little at a time, gently folding it with a spatula until just combined. **If you're making a mousse cake**, use the mousse immediately. **If you're making a layer cake**, refrigerate the mousse covered with plastic wrap pressed directly against the surface, until spreadable, about 5 minutes.

STORAGE

If you are using the mousse as a filling to build a cake, you will need to use it right away as it sets.

If you are ejoying the mousse on its own, once set, it can be refrigerated with plastic wrap pressed directly against the surface to prevent a skin from forming for up to 4 days.

BEST FOR

> Mousse cake

> On its own: I like to pour mousse into small cups or ramekins, chill it for at least 45 minutes to an hour, then top it with whipped cream for an easy dessert

CHOCOLATE CHAMPAGNE PEAR CAKE
BASE: Chocolate Cake (page 22)
FILLING: Dark Chocolate Champagne Mousse (page 204) + Pear Compote (page 151)
FINISHING: Caramelized Pears (page 241) + Chocolate Buttercream (page 222)
TECHNIQUE: How to Assemble a Mousse Cake (page 299)

MILK CHOCOLATE MOUSSE

FILLING

MY GO-TO DARK CHOCOLATE MOUSSE

Milk chocolate often gets a bad rap when compared to dark chocolate, but I find it is often a better accompaniment to softer and more subtle flavors that can be easily overwhelmed by dark chocolate. My favorite type of milk chocolate is gianduja, a soft milk chocolate made with hazelnut paste. If you see it, buy plenty of it—it's addictive.

THE CHANGE

Prepare **My Go-To Dark Chocolate Mousse** (page 200) as directed, but replace the dark chocolate with **305 grams (11 ounces) milk chocolate, chopped**, or **305 grams (11 ounces) gianduja, chopped**.

DARK CHOCOLATE CHAMPAGNE MOUSSE

FILLING

MY GO-TO DARK CHOCOLATE MOUSSE

Champagne is an elegant way to elevate a chocolate mousse, and it lightens the mousse's already airy texture. During the holidays, if you happen to have extra bubbly left over from a party, don't toss it—use it for this recipe!

THE CHANGE

In step 3 of **My Go-To Dark Chocolate Mousse** (page 200), add **100 grams (½ cup) Champagne (or cava, prosecco, or sparkling rosé)** to the ganache and stir until incorporated. Proceed with the recipe as directed.

RASPBERRY DARK CHOCOLATE MOUSSE

MY GO-TO DARK CHOCOLATE MOUSSE

I love the combination of chocolate and raspberry. The addition of a bright raspberry purée to a rich, chocolaty mousse makes a decadent and bright dessert.

THE CHANGE

In step 3 of **My Go-To Dark Chocolate Mousse** (page 200), add **50 grams (¼ cup) raspberry purée*** to the ganache and stir until incorporated. Proceed with the recipe as directed.

* *Prepared raspberry purée can be found in specialty stores and online. To make your own, in a blender, purée 50 grams (about ½ cup) fresh raspberries until smooth. If you like the seeds (which I do), there's no need to strain the purée. Otherwise, strain it through a fine-mesh sieve.*

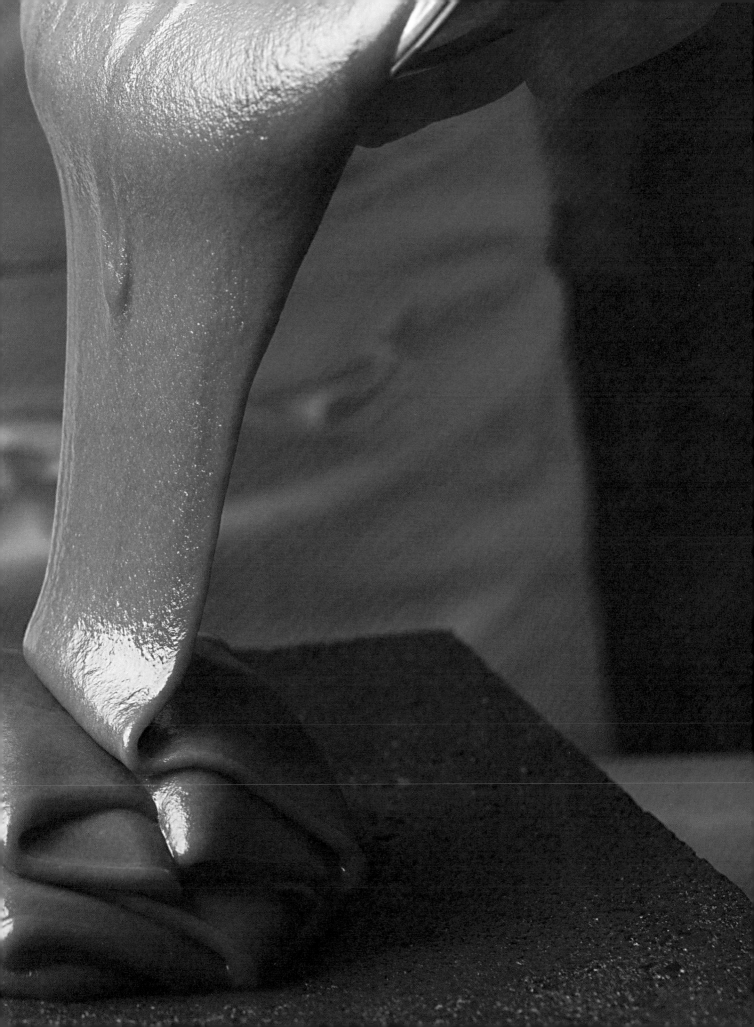

MY GO-TO SOFT CARAMEL

The best thing about this caramel is its texture—rich, smooth, a little chewy, and very satisfying. It instantly adds an ooey-gooey factor that I love in desserts. Use it sparingly, though. You don't want to overwhelm, just add a drizzle of decadence.

MAKES: 675 grams (2¾ cups), enough to fill two 8-inch tarts or one three-layered 8-inch or 20 cm cake, with leftover caramel

TIME: 45 minutes

INGREDIENTS

320 grams	1½ cups	heavy cream
200 grams	⅔ cup	light corn syrup
50 grams	¼ cup	dark brown sugar
100 grams	½ cup	granulated sugar
4 grams	½ teaspoon	fleur de sel

EQUIPMENT
Digital thermometer

1. **Make the cream mixture:** Whisk together the cream, corn syrup, and brown sugar in a small saucepan. Bring to a boil over medium heat. Remove from the heat and cover to keep warm.

2. **Make the dry caramel:** Place another small saucepan over medium heat. When the pan is hot, sprinkle a thin, even layer of the granulated sugar over the bottom of the pan. As the sugar melts and caramelizes, slowly whisk in the rest of the sugar, one handful at a time, making sure each handful of sugar has reached an amber brown color before adding another handful. Once all the sugar has been added, cook until it has turned golden amber brown, 1 to 2 minutes.* Remove from the heat immediately to keep it from burning.

   * *You can move the saucepan on and off the heat to control the temperature and make sure the sugar doesn't burn.*

3. **Combine the caramel and the cream mixture:** While whisking, slowly pour one-third of the warm cream mixture into the caramel and whisk until incorporated. Be careful, as the caramel might bubble and splatter as you add the cream. Whisk in half the remaining cream mixture until incorporated, then whisk in the remainder.* Clip a

digital thermometer to the side of the pan. Reduce the heat to low and cook, whisking continuously, until the caramel reaches 221°F (105°C), 4 to 5 minutes. Remove from the heat.

> * A whisk works well here, but you can use a hand blender instead to give your caramel an even smoother consistency.

4. Finish the caramel: Whisk in the fleur de sel. Pour the caramel into a large heatproof bowl and let cool completely. Once cool, stir well to re-emulsify any fat that has separated.

STORAGE

The caramel can be stored in an airtight container in the refrigerator for up to 3 days. Let the caramel sit at room temperature for 10 to 15 minutes and stir with a spatula to soften it before using.

BEST FOR

> Filling tarts
> Filling sandwich cookies
> Glazing brownies

ROSE OR GRAPPA FLAVORED SOFT CARAMEL

FILLING
MY GO-TO SOFT CARAMEL

Flavor soft caramel with ingredients like rose or grappa.

THE CHANGE

Prepare **My Go-To Soft Caramel** (page 208) as directed, then add **a few drops of rose extract (to taste)** or **50 grams (¼ cup) grappa** and stir with a spatula until combined.

PASSION FRUIT SOFT CARAMEL

FILLING
MY GO-TO SOFT CARAMEL

Passion fruit's light floral flavor gives this caramel a special and unexpected twist.

THE CHANGE

In step 1 of **My Go-To Soft Caramel** (page 208), whisk **120 grams (½ cup) passion fruit purée or juice** into the cream mixture before bringing it to a boil. Proceed with the recipe as directed. Because there's more liquid in this variation, you may need to cook it for 1 to 2 minutes longer.

LEMONGRASS SOFT CARAMEL

Citrus aromatics work well on caramel: they serve as a foil for its buttery and deep flavor. I first tried lemongrass caramel drizzled over coconut ice cream and instantly fell in love with the subtle twist.

THE CHANGE

In step 1 of **My Go-To Soft Caramel** (page 208), put the cream in a medium saucepan and bring to a boil over medium heat. Remove from the heat and add **50 grams (¾ cup) chopped fresh lemongrass**.* Cover the saucepan with a lid or plastic wrap and let stand for 20 minutes to infuse. Strain the cream through a fine-mesh sieve; discard the lemongrass. Return the cream to the pan, whisk in the corn syrup and brown sugar, and proceed with the recipe as directed.

> * To bring out the natural oils in the fresh lemongrass, hit the stalk with the back of a spoon before chopping.

FINISHINGS

Here's one of my favorite quotes from Julia Child:

"A party without a cake is just a meeting."

Desserts make the occasion. And so when it comes to finishing, the final step, dress up your dessert for the occasion. It's a party, after all.

Take a moment before and think. There's no more active work, no more mixing and baking and stacking. What's left to do requires finesse. And as much as this is the last touch for your dessert, remember that it will make the first impression on your guests. Greet them well.

The Croissant Test, and How Creativity Could Mean Getting Lost

Any young chef above *chef de partie* level must pass a test to work in any one of our kitchens around the world. As part of the interview process, she or he must bake three pastries: a tart, an *entrêmet* (mousse cake), and a croissant. The tart should be a beautiful canvas for berries piled up high or slices of apple and pear fanned out delicately atop a soft cream filling held within a thin, crumbly tart shell. The entrêmet should be carefully constructed with even layers of cake and mousse, each with its own unique flavor and texture, then glazed with a seamless layer of nappage or ganache. But of the three, none is more important to conquer than the humble croissant. Flour, butter, sugar, salt, and yeast: These five ingredients determine the fate of each and every pastry chef. Here is what I look for in the Croissant Test.

First, I examine the size and weight of the croissant. I like to eat croissants that are almost too big to hold with one hand. A croissant isn't intended to be a small bite or a canapé—it should be a meal in itself and needs to leave you satisfied. Beyond that, a generous size also prevents the crumb from drying out as quickly, since there's more mass to keep in the moisture.

Next, I examine the shape: Is the croissant rolled tightly so it doesn't unravel? Does it rise, proudly, in the center with a tall peak rather than what we call a flabby shape? As I pick it up, I look for a weight that is deceptively light for its size, a hint of the air pocket and layers within. By now, I already know whether the croissant has potential.

And then, the dreaded center cut: as I draw a serrated knife delicately through the croissant, young chefs hold their breath. The inside of the croissant should reveal even layers of pastry in a spiral pattern we call the honeycomb.

After slicing it open, I lean in to smell the croissant. It should smell slightly yeasty and sour; fermentation inside the dough gives the croissant a deep and complex flavor. Few people realize you need acid from the fermentation of the yeast to really highlight the sweetness and buttery notes of the dough.

Finally, I take a bite. The crust of the croissant should shatter as I bite down, the confetti of crumbs falling everywhere.

If the pastry holds up to each of these requirements, the young chef passes the Croissant Test. We let out a simultaneous sigh—for the candidate, it's one of relief; for me, one of satisfaction.

But things don't always go as planned. Over the years, I've seen all types of croissants, good and bad. There was a period of time when I tasted many flavored croissants—filled with bacon or apple pie filling or even cake frosting, all of which ripped through and destroyed the honeycomb within and had such overpowering flavors that you could barely detect the precious taste of the croissant.

One day, a candidate unveiled a "croissant panini." He had baked a ham-and-cheese croissant, slid it into a sandwich press, then crushed it down. I asked him why he went to the trouble of building layer upon layer of pastry, only to destroy his work. He looked at me in shock. And then he closed his eyes and, obviously disappointed in himself, whispered that he had forgotten what a good croissant was supposed to be.

Creativity requires us to wander off track, to break out of boundaries and explore new worlds. But we can—and often do—get lost. It's important to take the time to remind ourselves which way is due north. Never forget the lesson of the croissant, and the "croissant panini." Just because it hasn't been done before doesn't mean it's worth doing.

I recently visited the young chef who had failed our Croissant Test with his "panini-ed" rendition years ago. He has continued his pastry training and improved over time, and the croissant he presented me this time around incorporated the lessons I had taught him. He handed over a serrated knife and asked me for a cross-section test. I smiled. "Are you still holding your breath?" I asked.

MY GO-TO BUTTERCREAM

In the French kitchens where I learned to bake, we seldom frosted a cake with buttercream. But when I came to America, buttercream was often requested, and I learned to love its consistency: smooth and creamy, easy to spread on a cake. But I have to admit that I never learned to love its taste.

When I started to develop my recipe for buttercream, I wanted to see if I could improve on that taste. Typically, buttercream is made with softened butter and confectioners' sugar, whipped until light and fluffy. But I didn't like the taste of so much butter, which was heavy on my tongue, or the confectioners' sugar, so sweet it was almost cloying. My recipe is made with a sabayon, in which egg yolks and sugar are slowly combined to create a silky custard and softened butter is added at the end. The result is not only a better taste, but an even better consistency. This is a lighter, fluffier buttercream.

MAKES: 450 grams (2 cups), enough to frost an 8-inch or 20 cm two-layer cake
TIME: 30 minutes

INGREDIENTS

130 grams	⅔ cup	granulated sugar
45 grams	3 tablespoons	water
100 grams	6 large	egg yolks
450 grams	2 cups	unsalted butter, at room temperature

EQUIPMENT
Stand mixer with whisk attachment
Digital thermometer

1. Make the simple syrup: Combine the sugar and water in a medium saucepan and clip a digital thermometer to the side of the pan. Bring to a simmer over medium heat, whisking until the sugar has dissolved, then cook until the syrup reaches 250°F (121°C), 10 to 15 minutes. Remove from the heat.

2. Make the sabayon: Place the egg yolks in the bowl of stand mixer fitted with the whisk attachment. Whip the egg yolks on high speed. With the mixer running, slowly pour in the hot simple syrup on the side close to the bowl, avoiding the whisk attachment as best you can, and whip until the mixture is pale, fluffy, and thick and has increased in volume, 5 to 7 minutes. Turn off the mixer and let the sabayon cool completely.

3. Finish the buttercream: With the mixer on low, add the butter to the sabayon a little bit at a time and whip until fully incorporated.* The buttercream should be silky and smooth.

   * *Don't worry if the butter and sabayon don't immediately incorporate and looks a bit curdled. Keep whisking and the buttercream will eventually come together.*

STORAGE

The buttercream can be stored in an airtight container in the refrigerator for 2 to 3 days. To use, bring the buttercream to room temperature, then whisk in a stand mixer until spreadable.

BEST FOR

> Layered cakes. I wouldn't use it for mousse cakes, which are lighter and can be overpowered by buttercream.

FLAVORED BUTTERCREAM

Buttercreams are easy to flavor simply by whisking in the added ingredient as the final step. Even though it registers very delicately in the buttercream, I always think it's nice to make all components of the cake taste as good on their own as they do when combined with others.

THE CHANGE

Prepare **My Go-To Buttercream** (page 220) as directed, then add **50 grams (2 ounces) melted milk chocolate or dark chocolate,*** **50 grams (¼ cup) room-temperature cream cheese, or 10 grams (5 teaspoons) finely ground instant coffee** and whip the buttercream on low speed until combined. Stop to scrape down the sides as needed to make sure the added ingredient is fully incorporated.

> * *To melt the chocolate, finely chop it (if it isn't already in chips or small pieces), then place it in a medium heatproof bowl. Microwave it in 10- to 15-second intervals, stirring after each to prevent burning, until completely melted and smooth, but not too hot.*

MY GO-TO
NAPPAGE GLAZE

"Nappage" sounds fancy but is easy to make. Think of nappage as a protective neutral top coat for your desserts. To me, a tart isn't complete without nappage, especially since it helps prevent the cut surfaces of fresh fruits from browning over time. The nappage itself is only slightly sweet and doesn't carry very much flavor. But it's not to be missed if you're serious about presentation.

MAKES: 500 grams (2 cups), enough to glaze an 8-inch or 20 cm cake, with leftover glaze
TIME: 15 minutes

INGREDIENTS

150 grams	¾ cup	granulated sugar
345 grams	1½ cups	water
15 grams	1 tablespoon + ¾ teaspoon	pectin NH*

* It's important to use pectin NH for this recipe. It's a type of pectin that's thermally reversible, meaning it can be set, melted, and set again. Apple pectin will not work.

EQUIPMENT
Pastry brush

1. Make the simple syrup: Combine about half the sugar and the water in a medium saucepan and bring to a boil over medium heat. Remove from the heat.

2. Make the pectin mixture: Whisk together the remaining sugar and the pectin in a small bowl until combined.

3. Finish the nappage: Sprinkle the pectin mixture over the simple syrup and whisk until the sugar and pectin have dissolved.* Bring the mixture to a boil over medium heat. Cook for 2 minutes, then remove from the heat. Let cool for 10 to 15 minutes before using or storing.

* Combining the pectin with some of the sugar before sprinkling it over the simple syrup prevents it from clumping.

STORAGE

The nappage can be stored in an airtight container in the refrigerator for up to 1 week. To use, microwave the nappage until it's hot and pourable, with a consistency similar to warm maple syrup (add a little water to loosen it up if it's too thick), about 30 seconds. If the nappage has separated, blend it using a hand blender for a few seconds to combine, then tap the container on the counter a few times to remove any air bubbles that may have formed during blending.

BEST FOR

> Any dessert with fresh fruit as décor, especially fresh fruit tarts; with a pastry brush, lightly brush a thin layer of Nappage glaze to cover the fruits completely.

FRUIT PURÉE NAPPAGE GLAZE

Flavor basic nappage with puréed fruit, simply by whisking in the ingredient as the final step. Strawberries or raspberries work best here, as their red color will give your dessert a vibrant finish.

THE CHANGE

Prepare **My Go-To Nappage Glaze** (page 223) as directed, but before cooling, whisk in **50 grams (¼ cup) strawberry or raspberry purée*** until well combined. Bring the nappage back to a boil over medium heat and cook for 1 minute. Remove from the heat and let cool for 10 to 15 minutes before using.

> * *Prepared strawberry purée and raspberry purée can be found in specialty stores and online. To make your own, in a blender, purée 50 grams (½ cup) fresh strawberries or raspberries until smooth. Strain the purée through a fine-mesh sieve to remove the seeds.*

CARAMEL GLAZE

Adding caramel to My Go-To Nappage Glaze gives it an extra note of warmth, perfect for a banana or apple tart.

INGREDIENT

| 100 grams | ½ cup | granulated sugar |

ADDED EQUIPMENT

Silicone baking mat (or parchment paper)

THE CHANGE

1. **Make the nappage:** Prepare **My Go-To Nappage Glaze** (page 223) as directed and keep it warm over very low heat.

2. **Make the dry caramel:** Place a small saucepan over medium heat. When the pan is hot, sprinkle a thin, even layer of the sugar over the bottom of the pan. As the sugar melts and caramelizes, slowly whisk in a bit more of the sugar, one handful at a time, making sure each handful of sugar has reached an amber brown color before adding another handful. Once all the sugar has been added, cook until it has turned golden amber brown, 1 to 2 minutes, continually whisking.* Remove from the heat immediately to keep it from burning.

   * *You can move the saucepan on and off the heat to control the temperature and make sure the sugar doesn't burn.*

3. **Combine the caramel and the nappage:** Add the caramel to the warm nappage and stir to combine.

MY GO-TO DARK CHOCOLATE GLAZE

There's something mesmerizing about the way a glaze falls slowly over a cake, draping it like a blanket. When I first tried it as a culinary student, I carefully poured my glazes around the cake at different angles, but time and time again, I failed to deliver an even layer. I remember apologizing to the chef, until he finally revealed his secret: Glazing demands certainty. You can't hesitate. Take a deep breath, pour your glaze in one swift motion over the center of the cake, and trust that it'll go where it should.

MAKES: 500 grams (2 cups), enough to glaze an 8-inch or 20 cm cake, with leftover glaze
TIME: 30 minutes

INGREDIENTS

12 grams	4 teaspoons	unflavored powdered gelatin
60 grams	¼ cup	cold water for gelatin
70 grams	½ cup + 2 tablespoons	unsweetened cocoa powder
75 grams	⅓ cup	room-temperature water for cocoa powder
200 grams	1 cup	granulated sugar
140 grams	½ cup + 1½ tablespoons	heavy cream

EQUIPMENT

Digital thermometer
Fine-mesh sieve
Hand blender

1. Dissolve the gelatin: Combine the gelatin and 60 grams (¼ cup) cold water in a small bowl and stir with a spoon until the gelatin has dissolved.

2. Make the cocoa powder mixture: In a small bowl, whisk together the cocoa powder and 75 grams (⅓ cup) water until combined.

3. Make the glaze: Combine the sugar and cream in a medium saucepan and clip a digital thermometer to the side of the pan. Bring to a simmer over medium heat, whisking until the sugar has dissolved. Add the cocoa powder mixture and bring to a boil, whisking occasionally. Cook until the glaze reaches 113° to 122°F (45° to 50°C), about 5 minutes. Remove from the heat.

4. Finish the glaze: Set a fine-mesh sieve over the bowl with the gelatin mixture. Pour the glaze through the sieve, then whisk to combine with the gelatin mixture. Blend with a hand blender to remove any lumps.

STORAGE

The glaze can be stored in an airtight container in the refrigerator for up to 1 week. To use, microwave the glaze until it's hot and pourable (add a little water to loosen it up if it's too thick). If the glaze has separated, blend it using a hand blender for a few seconds to combine, then tap the container on the counter a few times to remove any air bubbles that may have formed during blending.

BEST FOR

> Glazing mousse cakes, éclairs, or cream puffs

MY GO-TO
WHITE CHOCOLATE GLAZE

Extra-glossy glazes, like this one, are sometimes called mirror glazes because you can see your reflection in them. This white chocolate glaze will give your mousse cake a mirrorlike finish with an ivory sheen.

MAKES: 500 grams (2 cups), enough to glaze an 8-inch or 20 cm cake, with leftover glaze
TIME: 30 minutes

INGREDIENTS

8 grams	2½ teaspoons	unflavored powdered gelatin
45 grams	3 tablespoons	cold water for gelatin
115 grams	⅓ cup	glucose
115 grams	½ cup + 4 teaspoons	granulated sugar
60 grams	¼ cup	room-temperature water for the glucose
75 grams	¼ cup	condensed milk
75 grams	½ cup	chopped white chocolate

EQUIPMENT
Digital thermometer
Hand blender

1. **Dissolve the gelatin:** Combine the gelatin and 45 grams (3 tablespoons) cold water in a small bowl and stir with a spoon until the gelatin has dissolved.

2. **Make the syrup:** Combine the glucose, sugar, and 60 grams (¼ cup) water in a medium saucepan and clip a digital thermometer to the side of the pan. Bring to a boil over high heat. Cook until the mixture reaches 113° to 122°F (45° to 50°C), about 10 minutes. Stir in the gelatin mixture with a spatula until incorporated. Remove from the heat.

3. **Make the glaze:** Combine the condensed milk and white chocolate in a large heatproof bowl. Pour the warm syrup over the chocolate, then stir with a spatula until the chocolate has melted and the glaze is smooth. Blend the glaze with a hand blender to remove any lumps.

STORAGE

The glaze can be stored in an airtight container in the refrigerator for up to 1 week. To use, microwave the glaze until it's hot and pourable (add a little water to loosen it up if it's too thick). If the glaze has separated, blend using a hand blender for a few seconds to combine, then tap the container on the counter a few times to remove any air bubbles that may have formed during blending.

BEST FOR

> Mousse cakes

BANANA BREAD WITH CHESTNUT-WHISKEY CHANTILLY CREAM
BASE: Banana Bread (page 60)
FINISHING: Caramelized Bananas (page 238) +
Chestnut-Whiskey Chantilly Cream (page 253)

MY GO-TO CARAMELIZED BANANAS

You might wonder, what's the difference between roasted fruit and caramelized fruit? Roasted fruits are cooked until thoroughly softened, and have a concentrated, almost jammy flavor. Caramelized fruits are cooked until golden on the outside but still firm. How flavors change, depends on how you choose to cook an ingredient!

The first time I tried caramelized bananas, they were ladled over a crepe, and I can still smell their burnt sugar, which had an almost bitter taste that melted away as I chewed.

MAKES: 500 grams (1 cup), enough to cover one 8-inch or 20 cm tart
TIME: 20 minutes

INGREDIENTS

100 grams	½ cup	granulated sugar
	4	bananas, peeled and sliced into 1-inch-thick (2.5 cm) coins
30 grams	2 tablespoons	unsalted butter

1. **Make the dry caramel:** Place a small nonstick pan over medium heat. When the pan is hot, sprinkle the sugar in an even layer over the bottom of the pan. Cook, stirring with a wooden spoon, until the sugar is blond in color, 1 to 2 minutes.

2. **Caramelize the bananas:** Place the bananas in the pan in an even layer. Cook for 1 minute, then flip and cook for 1 minute more, until the bananas are soft but not overly mushy.

3. **Deglaze the pan:** Add the butter and let it melt, swirling the pan and stirring as it melts to deglaze the pan.*

   * *Don't be intimidated—this isn't deglazing with alcohol like on TV, so you won't see a giant flambé flame in your kitchen. Here you're simply deglazing the pan with a bit of liquid—in this case, the moisture in the butter—to help lift the caramelized bananas from the bottom of the pan and prevent them from burning.*

4. Transfer the bananas to a large plate, placing them in an even layer, and let cool.*

   * *Don't forget all the other good stuff in the pan—scrape any leftover caramel into an airtight container and let it cool, too, then drizzle over ice cream or pour into your coffee.*

STORAGE

The caramelized bananas can be stored in an airtight container in the refrigerator for up to 3 days.

BEST FOR

> - I love these on a simple tart or a chocolate mousse cake
> - Leftover caramelized bananas are delicious over yogurt or ice cream

CARAMELIZED APPLES

FINISHING

**MY GO-TO
CARAMELIZED
BANANAS**

I grew up near Normandie, in the north of France, where apples are the number one choice of fruit for just about any dessert. Luckily, I love apples any time of year. Different varieties of apples have different flavors and textures, so it's important to choose apples that are good for baking—these varieties won't turn to mush. My favorites are Honeycrisp and Gala.

INGREDIENTS

100 grams	½ cup	granulated sugar
	4	Honeycrisp or Gala apples, peeled, cored, and cut into 8 wedges each
60 grams	¼ cup	Calvados or apple brandy

THE CHANGE

1. Make the dry caramel: Place a small nonstick pan over medium heat. When the pan is hot, sprinkle the sugar in an even layer over the bottom of the pan. Cook, stirring with a wooden spoon, until the sugar is blond in color, 1 to 2 minutes.

2. Caramelize the apples: Place the apples in the pan in an even layer. On medium heat, cook for 1 to 2 minutes, then flip and cook for 1 to 2 minutes more, until the apples are tender but not mushy (whether it takes 1 or 2 minutes to achieve this texture will depend on the variety of apple used).

3. Deglaze the pan: Remove the pan from the heat (this is very important for safety). Holding the pan well away from your body, add the Calvados to the pan. Raise the heat to high, return the pan to the heat, and shake the pan slightly. As the alcohol heats, it will ignite, and you'll see some small blue flames on the apples; these will burn out after a few seconds as the alcohol cooks off. Cook on low to medium heat until the apples are tender, 15 to 20 minutes.

4. Transfer the apples to a large plate, placing them in an even layer, and let cool.*

> * *Don't forget all the other good stuff in the pan—scrape any leftover caramel into an airtight container and let it cool, too, then drizzle over ice cream or pour into your coffee.*

CARAMELIZED PEARS

I love baking with fresh pears when the weather turns cool. There are lots of different ways to prepare them—grilled, poached, caramelized, or simply sliced and enjoyed fresh. Bosc and Williams pears are two of the most common varieties, and they both keep their texture when baked.

INGREDIENTS

100 grams	½ cup	granulated sugar
	4	Bosc or Williams pears, peeled, cored, and cut into 8 wedges each
4 grams	2 teaspoons	ground cinnamon*
4 grams	2 teaspoons	ground ginger

* A few years ago, I discovered Vietnamese cinnamon, which is a lot more fragrant than standard ground cinnamon. If you have access to it or spot a jar in the market, I highly recommend buying it!

THE CHANGE

1. Make the dry caramel: Place a small nonstick pan over medium heat. When the pan is hot, sprinkle the sugar in an even layer over the bottom of the pan. Cook, stirring with a wooden spoon, until the sugar is blond in color, 1 to 2 minutes.

2. Caramelize the pears: Place the pears in the pan in an even layer. On medium heat, cook for 1 to 2 minutes, then flip and cook for 15 to 20 minutes more, until the pears are tender but not mushy (how long it takes will depend on the variety of pear used and its ripeness). If they seem to be getting too soft on the outside but are not cooked through yet, add a tiny bit of water to help them cook more evenly. Sprinkle the pears with the cinnamon and ginger and stir gently to combine.

3. Transfer the pears to a large plate, placing them in an even layer, and let cool.*

* Don't forget all the other good stuff in the pan—scrape any leftover caramel into an airtight container and let it cool, too, then drizzle over ice cream or pour into your coffee.

CARAMELIZED PEACHES

Peaches are one of my favorite summer fruits. They're fragrant, sweet, and juicy—and especially good for baking, as they hold their shape when caramelized, even in pies and tarts. Yellow and white peaches both work here, but I love donut peaches and nectarines, too.

INGREDIENTS

100 grams	½ cup	granulated sugar*
	4	peaches, pitted, and cut into 8 wedges each
30 grams	2 tablespoons	unsalted butter
	4 sprigs	lemon thyme

* *You can also skip making the caramel and use honey in the same proportion. Simply heat the honey in a pan over medium heat until it is liquid and just bubbling. Then add the peaches and proceed as directed. I like using clover honey.*

THE CHANGE

1. Make the dry caramel: Place a large nonstick pan over medium heat. Using a large pan will help prevent over-crowding for your fruit. When the pan is hot, sprinkle the sugar in an even layer over the bottom of the pan. Cook, stirring continuously with a wooden spoon, until the sugar is blond in color, 1 to 2 minutes.

2. Caramelize the peaches: Place the peaches in the pan in an even layer. Cook for 1 to 2 minutes, then flip and cook for 1 to 2 minutes more, until the peaches are tender but not mushy (whether it takes 1 or 2 minutes to achieve this texture will depend on the variety of peach used). Transfer the peaches to a large plate and remove their skins, then return them to the pan.

3. Deglaze the pan: Add the butter to the pan, then add the lemon thyme sprigs.* Swirl the pan and stir as the butter melts to deglaze the pan.

* *Don't add the lemon thyme too early, as it'll burn. It should cook for less than 1 minute so add when the butter is just almost melted.*

4. Transfer the peaches to a large plate, placing them in an even layer, and let cool. Discard the lemon thyme sprigs.*

* *Don't forget all the other good stuff in the pan—scrape any leftover caramel into an airtight container and let it cool, too, then drizzle over ice cream or pour into your coffee.*

MY GO-TO ROASTED FRUITS

Pastry chefs pay attention to the weather, because which fruits are in season affects what we can bake. In the spring, when certain fruits are just starting to ripen, I get impatient. I speed up the process of fruits' ripening by roasting them in the oven, which concentrates their flavor when the sun is away.

MAKES: 500 grams (2 cups), enough to cover one 8-inch or 20 cm tart
TIME: 30 minutes

FIGS AND BALSAMIC
500 grams	2¼ cups	black Mission figs
		drizzle of balsamic vinegar
		sprinkle of granulated sugar

APRICOTS AND HONEY
| 500 grams | 2½ cups | fresh apricots, pitted |
| | | drizzle of honey |

PINEAPPLE AND BROWN SUGAR
| 500 grams | 2 cups | diced fresh pineapple |
| | | sprinkle of dark brown sugar |

For an added twist, toss the fruit with fresh herbs like rosemary, thyme, or tarragon. I especially love mixing herbs with stone fruits. You could also add spices; cinnamon and cloves work well with acidic fruits like pineapple.

1. **Preheat the oven:** Preheat the oven to 350°F (175°C).

2. **Combine the ingredients:** Combine all the ingredients in a large bowl and toss with a spatula or your hands until the fruit is evenly coated.

3. **Roast the fruit:** Arrange the fruit on a sheet pan in an even layer. Roast, stirring occasionally with a spatula to prevent burning, until the fruit is tender, 10 to 15 minutes, depending on the ripeness, size, and type of fruit. Check on the fruit often rather than use a timer.

STORAGE

The roasted fruit is best used right away, but can be cooled completely and stored in an airtight container in the refrigerator for up to 3 days.

BEST FOR

> Tarts

> Topped with streusel and served with ice cream

MY GO-TO
FRESH FRUITS

Few things can compete with fresh fruit at the peak of its season. It packs more flavor in one bite than many dessert components. Sometimes I find myself snacking on the cut fruits and realize I've eaten so much that there's not enough fruit left to cover my tart.

MAKES: 500 grams (2 cups), enough to cover one 8-inch or 20 cm tart
TIME: 15 minutes

INGREDIENTS
Fruit of your choice

SEASONALITY AND RIPENESS

Whenever possible, use ripe, in-season fruits, and even better if they're locally grown. If you have a farmers' market nearby, the fruits on display will most likely be what's in season in your area. A fruit may be in season at different times of year depending on the geographic location in which its grown: strawberries, for example, are plentiful in France in the summer, but are a winter fruit in Japan.

Every fruit has its own signs of ripeness, but my three-step test is:

1. Look at the color of the fruit: Ripe fruits tend to be more vibrant.

2. Touch the fruit to determine how firm it is: When pressed gently, most fruits feel soft when ripe.

3. Smell the fruit: Ripe fruits smell much stronger than unripe ones.

VARIETIES

All varieties of fruit are suitable for topping cakes and tarts. But juicier ones, like oranges or grapefruits, do need to be drained on a paper towel for a few minutes before you place them on a cake or tart. Some of my favorite fruits to use to top tarts are:

> Berries
> Citrus (grapefruit, orange)
> Exotic fruits (lychee, guava, papaya)
> Figs
> Mangoes
> Pineapple
> Stone fruits (plums, peaches, apricots, nectarines, cherries)

TIPS

> Wash and dry the fruit thoroughly before using.
> Peel the fruit if the skin is inedible, and core it if necessary.
> If you are keeping your fruit whole (i.e., berries), try to pick equal-size fruits for a more consistent topping on tarts.
> If you are cutting your fruit (i.e., peaches), wait until as close to serving time as possible to keep the fruit fresh and avoid oxidation, and make sure you use a sharp knife.
> Whatever fruit you choose, use plenty of it to top the tart, so each serving gets a generous portion.

MY GO-TO VANILLA CHANTILLY CREAM

Chantilly is, quite simply, a fancy term for whipped cream. But never underestimate how delicious simple whipped cream can be. That extra bit of Chantilly is the perfect finishing touch for everything from tarts to pavlovas, as it helps to harmonize flavors.

MAKES: 550 grams (4½ cups), enough for one 8-inch or 20 cm tart or one 8-inch or 20 cm cake, with leftover Chantilly

TIME: 10 minutes

INGREDIENTS

500 grams	2 cups + 2 tablespoons	cold heavy cream*
50 grams	¼ cup	granulated sugar
3 grams	½	Tahitian vanilla bean, split lengthwise, seeds scraped

* *Make sure your cream is cold. If it's room temperature or warm, it won't whip up into fluffy peaks.*

EQUIPMENT

Whisk (or a hand mixer or a stand mixer fitted with a whisk attachment)

In a stand mixer fitted with the whisk attachment (or in a large bowl using a hand mixer or a whisk), combine the cream, sugar, and vanilla seeds and whip until the cream holds soft peaks, 3 to 4 minutes. If you are whisking by hand, use a large metal bowl and steadily whisk for roughly 5 minutes until the cream reaches soft peaks.

STORAGE

The Chantilly cream can be stored in the refrigerator in an airtight container, with plastic wrap pressed against the surface of the Chantilly to prevent a skin from forming, for up to 3 days. You may need to whip the Chantilly again prior to using it if it has deflated.

BEST FOR

> Chantilly is light and an easy match with all flavors, but it is not as stable, making it not ideal for frosting cakes unless just before serving. However, it is a wonderful topping for a pavlova or a fresh fruit tart.

FLAVORED CHANTILLY CREAM

MY GO-TO VANILLA CHANTILLY CREAM

Flavor My Go-To Vanilla Chantilly Cream with ingredients like chestnut and whiskey, Greek yogurt, pistachio paste, or tarragon leaves, simply by folding in the ingredient with a spatula as the final step.

CHESTNUT-WHISKEY CHANTILLY CREAM

| 25 grams | 1½ tablespoons | chestnut paste (it's easy to order online) |
| 5 grams | 1 teaspoon | whiskey |

GREEK YOGURT CHANTILLY CREAM

| 50 grams | 3 tablespoons | plain Greek yogurt |

PISTACHIO CHANTILLY CREAM

| 25 grams | 1½ tablespoons | pistachio paste |

TARRAGON CHANTILLY CREAM

Leaves from 1 sprig fresh tarragon

THE CHANGE

Prepare **My Go-To Vanilla Chantilly Cream** (page 252) as directed, then add your desired flavorings and gently fold them in with a spatula until incorporated (be careful not to deflate the fluffy peaks).

Always Measure the Size of the Door

Once while living in Paris, I visited the Musée d'Orsay, which holds one of the largest collections of Impressionist and Postimpressionist paintings in the world. It was there that I first learned the story of Paul Cézanne. The painter, whose use of colors and brushstrokes captured the beauty of the French countryside, focused on simple subjects such as fruits and flowers in his still lifes. Even hanging on the cold museum walls, you can feel the warmth of the sun in Provence on his canvases. But he wasn't always so well-regarded.

And as I delved deeper into his story, I thought, *I know exactly how he felt.*

A few weeks before this visit, I was offered the opportunity to create a grand *pièce montée*, a centerpiece cake, for the wedding of a gypsy king. I happily accepted. The wedding would be taking place in a field where an entire structure had been built especially for the over one thousand attendees. It was the largest job that I had ever been asked to complete, and I was confident I was up to the task. The cake would be a masterpiece—toweringly tall, intricately decorated, and, of course, absolutely delicious.

The only problem was that I didn't know how I was actually going to build it. I could dream it, of course. But as a young chef, your ambition often overshadows your capabilities. The first challenge was that the soft mousse cake I had selected as a base did not make a strong foundation—at least, not on the scale I had intended. And no matter how many wooden support dials I used as support, the bottom layers of the vanilla sponge cake were on the verge of buckling under the added weight, which seemed to increase as the heat dragged down the ingredients even more. The intricate gold and silver decorations, each gently fashioned and attached to the white fondant covering the cake, began to melt in the humidity.

Looking back now, there were steps I would take to avoid these problems. I would have built a stand out of wood or plastic to elevate each layer of the cake, rather than stacking the layers directly on top of one another. I would not have decorated the cake so early. I would've thought about how long the cake would need to stand at room temperature. But I didn't know any of that back then. I was only in my twenties, and my ego had assured me that it would all work out. I struggled for days to build and rebuild the cake as the party edged ever closer. All I knew was that the ingredients, once seemingly full of potential, would no longer bend to my command.

Young Cézanne struggled for years in similar ways, staring at his canvas. You see, Cézanne wasn't very good at drawing. He signed up for night school and asked his friends and family to support him through his education. He twice applied to the famous Académie des Beaux-Arts (now the École des Beaux-Arts), and was twice rejected. Cézanne's now iconic paintings then only existed in his head. Chefs, like artists, want our creations to be awe-inspiring. But in the same way that Cézanne practiced for years before he could deliver what he imagined, the gap between thinking and doing can be a big one.

After struggling for days, I managed to patch together a somewhat passable cake. I drove at snail-speed to the wedding, protecting my precious cargo at each curve and bump in the road. When I arrived, three other chefs helped me carry it to the venue—only to discover it was too big to fit through the door!

Decades later, the memory of that moment still stings. Every failed test or unsuccessful creation can knock you off course. The key is to go back to the drawing board—or to the kitchen, in my case—and collect yourself. Research. Practice. Then keep going.

Cézanne famously recounted how he used to frequent the Louvre and copy the works by Michelangelo and other artists hanging on its walls. The first step is to accept that you may not know enough, and the next step is to embrace the fact that you can never know too much. It wasn't until he was in his fifties that Cézanne's paintings started looking the way he had always imagined. I, too, grew comfortable building large-scale cakes much later in my career. And nowadays, before I begin any big project, I always ask for the size of the door.

MY GO-TO ITALIAN MERINGUE (FOR PIPING AND FINISHING)

There are three basic types of meringue: French, Swiss, and Italian. French meringue uses raw egg whites, and is often later baked; it is the least stable of the three. Swiss meringue involves gently heating egg whites as you add sugar, which makes it both denser (and therefore more stable) and smoother than French meringue; it's usually mixed with other components, such as buttercream, and used to frost cakes. This recipe is for an Italian meringue, the most stable of the three types. It requires you to drizzle hot sugar syrup into egg whites as they're being whipped, resulting in tall, fluffy meringue peaks.

MAKES: 500 grams (2 cups), enough to top one 8-inch or 20 cm tart or cake, or to make one 8-inch or 20 cm pavlova, with leftover meringue

TIME: 15 to 20 minutes

INGREDIENTS

300 grams	1½ cups	granulated sugar
70 grams	⅓ cup	water
145 grams	5 large	egg whites*

* *One trick I always remember with eggs is the "30-20-10" rule. A large egg is generally about 60 grams in weight: the white is 30 grams, the yolk is 20 grams, the shell is 10 grams. It's always helpful to remember when a recipe calls for eggs in grams, like this one, for an estimate.*

EQUIPMENT

Digital thermometer

Stand mixer with whisk attachment (I don't recommend doing this by hand)

1. Make the sugar syrup: Combine the sugar and water in a small saucepan and clip a digital thermometer to the side of the pan. Cook over medium heat, stirring often, until the sugar syrup reaches 250°F (121°C).

2. Meanwhile, whip the egg whites: In a stand mixer fitted with the whisk attachment, whip the egg whites on medium speed until foamy.

3. Whip the meringue: As soon as the sugar syrup reaches 250°F (121°C), remove it from the heat. Increase the mixer speed to high and very slowly* pour the sugar syrup into the egg whites down the side of the mixer bowl, avoiding the whisk attachment as best you can. Whip until the meringue holds soft peaks (when you lift the whisk out of the bowl, the meringue should hold its shape), about 5 minutes; it should still be warm to the touch, which makes it easier to pipe. Use the meringue immediately; refrigerating will cause it to separate and deflate.*

  * *Make sure to pour in the sugar syrup very slowly, or it will cook the egg whites and the meringue will clump.*

  * *Tip: If you'd like, after spreading or piping the meringue, you can gently brown it with a small handheld butane torch; be sure to ignite the torch away from the meringue so the meringue doesn't end up tasting like butane. Holding the torch about 3 inches away from the surface of the meringue, gently pass the flame over the meringue until it reaches the desired golden brown color.*

STORAGE

Meringue should be used immediately to top your cake or tart.

BEST FOR

> Meringue is sweet, so it's best for desserts that use lots of fruit. I like it for tarts.

CHOCOLATE MERINGUE

Once you've mastered My Go-To Italian Meringue, you can modify it with many different flavors. But it's important to combine like with like: the texture of the added ingredient should match the texture of the meringue. For instance, for chocolate flavor, add melted chocolate rather than cocoa powder, which will clump.

MAKES: 550 grams meringue (2¼ cups), enough to top one 8-inch or 20 cm tart or cake, or to make one 8-inch or 20 cm pavlova, with leftover meringue

THE CHANGE

Prepare **My Go-To Italian Meringue** (page 258) as directed, then gently fold in **50 grams (2 ounces) melted dark or milk chocolate*** with a spatula until evenly distributed throughout the meringue—sometimes, I like to leave some streaks of chocolate visible. Mix gently so as not to deflate the meringue.

* *To melt the chocolate, finely chop it (if it isn't already in chips or small pieces), then place it in a medium heatproof bowl. Microwave it in 10- to 15-second intervals, stirring after each to prevent burning, until completely melted and smooth, but not too hot.*

EARL GREY ITALIAN MERINGUE

Earl Grey tea lends a fragrant flavor to classic Italian meringue.

MAKES: 500 grams (2 cups), enough to top one 8-inch or 20 cm tart or cake, or to make one 8-inch or 20 cm pavolva, with leftover meringue

THE CHANGE

Prepare **My Go-To Italian Meringue** (page 258) as directed, then gently fold in **2 grams (1 teaspoon) finely ground Earl Grey tea leaves** with a spatula until evenly distributed. Mix carefully so as not to deflate the meringue.

RASPBERRY MERINGUE

FINISHING

MY GO-TO ITALIAN MERINGUE

Fruit jams and compotes give your meringue a burst of fruit flavor. I love raspberry jam for its tartness, but strawberry jam, cherry jam, and citrus marmalade all also work well.

MAKES: 550 grams meringue (2¼ cups), enough to top one 8-inch or 20 cm tart or cake, or to make one 8-inch or 20 cm pavlova, with leftover meringue

THE CHANGE

Prepare **My Go-To Italian Meringue** (page 258) as directed, then gently fold in **50 grams (3 tablespoons) raspberry jam*** with a spatula until evenly distributed. Mix carefully so as not to deflate the meringue.

   * *You can make your own raspberry jam using the recipe on page 159, or use your favorite store-bought jam.*

EVERYONE CAN BAKE

264

TOASTED HAZELNUT MERINGUE

MY GO-TO ITALIAN MERINGUE

Folding toasted hazelnuts into creams, batters, and yes, meringues, lends a nutty flavor but also delivers a special crunch. You can also substitute almonds, pecans, or walnuts for the hazelnuts—whichever you choose, always toast them before adding them to your meringue. Raw nuts sometimes have a sharp, astringent flavor, and roasting mellows their bite—you're after subtlety here.

MAKES: 550 grams meringue (2¼ cups), enough to top one 8-inch or 20 cm tart cake, or to make one 8-inch or 20 cm pavlova, with leftover meringue

THE CHANGE

Prepare **My Go-To Italian Meringue** (page 258) as directed, then gently fold in **50 grams (½ cup) toasted finely chopped hazelnuts*** with a spatula until evenly distributed. Mix carefully so as not to deflate the meringue.

> * To toast your hazelnuts, spread them over a parchment paper–lined sheet pan and toast in a preheated 350°F (175°C) oven for 10 to 15 minutes, until they've browned lightly and you can smell their toasted nutty aroma. (Be sure not to burn them! It'll make your meringue taste bitter.) Let the nuts cool completely before adding them to your meringue.

MY GO-TO STREUSEL CRUMBLE

In my kitchens, I encourage aspiring pastry chefs to thinking about adding either flavor or texture when they create a dessert. Streusel adds both crunchiness and nuttiness. I love topping roasted stone fruits with handfuls of this.

MAKES: 1 kilogram (9 cups), enough to cover at least three 8-inch or 20 cm cakes, with plenty left over to snack on for breakfast
TIME: 45 minutes

INGREDIENTS

250 grams	2 cups	all-purpose flour
250 grams	2½ cups	hazelnut flour*
250 grams	1¼ cups	granulated sugar
6 grams	1½ teaspoons	fleur de sel
250 grams	2¼ sticks	unsalted butter, at room temperature

> * If you can't find hazelnut flour, pulse 250 grams (3 cups) whole hazelnuts in a food processor or blender until finely ground. You can also substitute almond, pistachio, or walnut flour.

EQUIPMENT
Stand mixer with paddle attachment (optional)

1. **Preheat the oven:** Preheat the oven to 350°F (175°C). Line a sheet pan with parchment paper.

2. **Make the streusel dough:** In a stand mixer fitted with the paddle attachment (or in a large bowl using a spatula), combine the all-purpose flour, hazelnut flour, sugar, and fleur de sel. Add the butter and mix to combine. Using your fingers, break up the streusel dough into pieces about the size of marbles. (Alternatively, push the dough through the holes of a wire rack to get pieces of a more uniform size.)

3. **Bake the streusel:** Spread the streusel over the prepared pan and bake until golden, 10 to 12 minutes. The edges should be crunchy and the inside still soft. Let cool completely.

STORAGE

The streusel can be stored in an airtight container at room temperature for up to 3 days.

BEST FOR

> Topping loaf cakes or tarts with roasted fruit
> Sprinkling on top of yogurt
> Topping roasted fruits, with a scoop of ice cream alongside

OAT STREUSEL CRUMBLE

Old-fashioned rolled oats give streusel even more texture and bite.

THE CHANGE

In step 2 of **My Go-To Streusel Crumble** (page 268), replace the hazelnut flour with **250 grams (2¾ cups) old-fashioned rolled oats** and the fleur de sel with **6 grams (1 tablespoon) orange zest**, and **add 40 grams (2 tablespoons) honey**. Proceed with the recipe as directed.

MY GO-TO VANILLA ICE CREAM

I believe that everything tastes a little better à la mode. I love the contrast of temperatures—a warm tart and a cold scoop of ice cream. My favorite flavor is vanilla. Use real vanilla beans and not extract. The signature, yet almost indescribable flavor is a blend of floral, woodsy and sweet—it's a classic for a reason.

MAKES: 1 liter (about 1 quart)
TIME: 1 hour, plus chilling overnight

INGREDIENTS

530 grams	2¼ cups	whole milk
170 grams	¾ cup	heavy cream
6 grams	1	Tahitian vanilla bean, split lengthwise, seeds scraped
100 grams	5 large	egg yolks
130 grams	⅔ cup	granulated sugar

EQUIPMENT
Fine-mesh sieve or hand blender
Ice cream machine

1. Make the warm milk mixture: Combine the milk, cream, and vanilla seeds in a medium saucepan and bring to a simmer over medium heat, stirring occasionally. Remove from the heat.

2. Make the egg yolk mixture: Whisk together the egg yolks and sugar in a medium bowl until fully combined.

3. Temper the egg yolk mixture: While whisking, slowly pour one-third of the warm milk mixture into the egg yolk mixture and whisk until fully incorporated to temper the eggs. Whisk in another third of the milk mixture, then pour the tempered egg mixture into the saucepan with the remaining milk mixture.

4. Make the crème anglaise: Cook the custard over medium heat, stirring continuously with a spatula, until it's thick enough to coat the back of the spatula, 4 to 5 minutes. (If you can swipe your finger through the custard on the back of the spatula and the line left by your finger remains, it's ready!) Remove from the heat.

5. Chill the crème anglaise: Fill a large bowl with ice and water. Strain the crème anglaise through a fine-mesh sieve into a medium bowl and place the bowl in the ice water. Slowly whisk the crème anglaise until chilled (this stops it from continuing to cook).*

> * *I like to refrigerate the crème anglaise overnight to intensify the vanilla flavor. Use plastic wrap pressed against the surface to prevent a skin from forming.*

6. Make the ice cream: Pour the crème anglaise into your ice cream machine and churn according to the manufacturer's instructions. Transfer the finished ice cream to an airtight 1-quart (1-liter) container and freeze until hardened to your liking before serving.

STORAGE

The ice cream can be stored in an airtight container in the freezer for up to 1 week.

BEST WITH

> Everything!

CHOCOLATE ICE CREAM

FINISHING

MY GO-TO VANILLA
ICE CREAM

Although I love vanilla ice cream, this rich and silky chocolate ice cream is a close second.

THE CHANGE

In step 1 of **My Go-To Vanilla Ice Cream** (page 274), omit the vanilla seeds. At the end of step 4, add **150 grams (6 ounces) finely chopped dark chocolate** to the crème anglaise while it is still warm and stir until the chocolate has melted and is fully incorporated. Proceed with the recipe as directed.

FRUIT SWIRL ICE CREAM

**MY GO-TO VANILLA
ICE CREAM**

To create a fruit swirl ice cream, start with My Go-To Vanilla Ice Cream recipe and add your favorite variation of My Go-To Stone Fruit Jam recipe. I love the small pieces of fruit that you discover in the bites and the slight variance in texture of the jam within the ice cream.

ADDED EQUIPMENT
Piping bag

THE CHANGE

1. Prepare **My Go-To Vanilla Ice Cream** (page 274) as directed, but after churning, do not remove it from the ice cream machine.

2. Fill a piping bag with 100 to 350 grams (½ cup to 1½ cups) fruit jam of your choice (see pages 156–163) and snip off the tip to make a ¼-inch (6 mm) opening.

3. Pack a layer of ice cream over the bottom of a 1-quart (1-liter) container. Pipe a thin layer of jam on top, then add more ice cream. Continue alternating layers of ice cream and jam. To swirl the jam into the ice cream, insert a skewer and draw a figure-8 pattern along the bottom of the container. Cover the container and freeze until hardened to your liking before serving.

SALTED CARAMEL
ICE CREAM

FINISHING

MY GO-TO VANILLA
ICE CREAM

Another favorite ice cream flavor is salted caramel. In this variation, the sugar that would otherwise sweeten the crème anglaise is used to make a caramel, which is then used to infuse the milk mixture with caramel flavor.

INGREDIENTS

200 grams (1 cup) granulated sugar

ADDED EQUIPMENT

Silicone baking mat (or parchment paper)

THE CHANGE

1. Make the dry caramel: Line a sheet pan with a silicone baking mat or parchment paper. Put **200 grams (1 cup) granulated sugar** in a small bowl and set it nearby. Place a small saucepan over medium heat. When the pan is hot, sprinkle a thin, even layer of the sugar over the bottom of the pan. As the sugar melts and caramelizes, slowly whisk in the rest of the sugar, one handful at a time, making sure each handful of sugar has reached an amber brown color before adding another handful. Once all the sugar has been added, cook until it has turned golden amber brown, 1 to 2 minutes.* Remove from the heat immediately to keep it from burning. Pour the caramel onto the prepared pan and set it aside to cool and harden for 10 to 15 minutes. Using the back of spoon, break the caramel into small pieces about the size of a potato chip.

> * *You can move the saucepan on and off the heat to control the temperature and make sure the sugar doesn't burn.*

2. Make the warm milk mixture: Follow as directed in step 1 of **My Go-To Vanilla Ice Cream** (page 274), but omit the vanilla seeds. Add the caramel pieces and stir until the caramel has melted and is fully incorporated into the milk mixture. Remove from the heat.

3. Make the egg yolk mixture: In step 2, omit the sugar and whisk just the egg yolks in a medium bowl, then temper the eggs with the warm milk mixture as directed in step 2. Proceed with the recipe as directed. When finished, I like to sprinkle a few flecks of coarse large salt crystals on top. Fleur de sel is a favorite, as is Maldon sea salt.

ASSEMBLY
&
TECHNIQUES

HOW TO FONÇAGE A TART SHELL

In one of my first tests in culinary school, I was asked to properly line a tart ring. *Le fonçage*, as the process is known, was a key task to separate the serious cooks from the amateurs. Too thick of a crust and it would be hard to cut your dessert with a fork. Too thin, and it would easily break and crumble. And even a small hole or tear in the dough would result in your tart filling leaking out. But with enough practice, it's easy to show off a beautifully fonçaged shell.

You can use this technique for any tart dough from the Bases chapter. Just make sure that the dough is completely chilled before you start; it should feel flexible but still form to the touch.

YOU'LL NEED

All-purpose flour, for dusting

1 disc of tart dough (see pages 4–15), well chilled

Butter, for the 8-inch (20 cm) tart ring

Tart ring*

> * *I prefer to use a straight-sided tart ring. Straight-sided tart shells bake more evenly than fluted ones. You can use a tart pan with a removable bottom instead of a tart ring, if you prefer.*

Dough scraper (optional)

1. Liberally flour your work surface and rolling pin. Place the chilled tart dough on your work surface and liberally flour the dough as well.

2. Start by pressing the rolling pin into the dough, going up and down the surface of the dough several times, to soften it. Then, applying even pressure, roll out the dough, starting from the center and rolling out toward the top and bottom.* Every 2 or 3 rolls, gently pick up the dough and rotate it a quarter turn. If the dough sticks to your work surface, gently run a dough scraper underneath it to help free it.* When the dough is uniformly about ⅛ inch (3 mm) thick, you're done rolling.

> * *It's important to work quickly so the dough does not warm up too much.*

> * *Feel free to add more flour to the surface or rolling pin as needed to prevent sticking. Don't worry—you can always brush off the excess so it is better to be safe than sorry.*

3. Place a tart ring in the center of the dough. Use a paring knife to cut a round of dough 1 inch (4 cm) wider than the tart ring.

4. Butter the tart ring. Line a sheet pan with parchment paper and set the tart ring in the pan.*

    * *If you're using a tart pan with a bottom, you can skip this step.*

5. Gently roll the dough over the rolling pin, lift it, and unroll it over the prepared tart ring.

6. Line the tart ring by gently using the side of your index finger to press the dough toward the bottom edge of the tart ring. Use your other hand to slightly lift the dough so it doesn't stretch.*

    * *Do not press the dough too hard against the side of the tart ring or the dough will thin out and your tart shell will bake unevenly (with the sides browning before the bottom is baked).*

7. Roll the rolling pin over the top of the tart ring, applying gentle pressure to cut away the excess dough hanging over the edge. If any overhanging dough remains, use a paring knife to trim it away evenly.*

    * *Lightly flour your knife blade to prevent the dough from sticking to it.*

8. If the dough has gotten warm as you've been working with it, return it to the refrigerator for 15 minutes before baking; warm or overworked dough will shrink as it bakes.

WHY I DON'T DOCK

Many of you may have heard of docking, the technique where you prick small holes in the dough for a tart shell or pie crust before baking. The holes help steam escape as the crust bakes, so it doesn't puff up. I prefer not to do this because liquid fillings will seep out of the holes. Instead, after I've fonçaged a tart shell (see page 282), I line it with parchment paper and fill it with dried beans or rice, then blind bake the tart shell for 20–25 minutes (see page 5). The weight of the dried beans or rice keeps the bottom of the tart shell flat, and there's no risk of filling seeping through later.

HOW TO BUILD A TART

Building a tart is much simpler than building a cake, but doing so perfectly requires understanding some subtle techniques.

YOU'LL NEED

1 blind-baked tart shell (pages 282–283), unmolded and cooled completely

Filling of your choice (pages 121–208)

Finishing(s) of your choice (pages 220–274)

Piping bag

Serrated knife (for serving the tart)

1. Set the tart shell on a flat plate or cake stand.

2. If you'll be filling the tart with a pastry cream or curd, let it come to room temperature, then whip it to make it smooth and fluffy. Transfer the filling to a piping bag and snip off the tip to make a small (about ½ inch or 1.5 cm) opening.*

> * *You could use a spatula to fill your tart, but I prefer to use a piping bag, especially for looser fillings, so that I have more control and the filling doesn't spill over the edges of the tart shell.*

3. Start by piping the filling around the inner edge of the tart shell, then spiral inward toward the center. Depending on how you decorate the tart, either fill it up to the rim or about ⅛ inch (3 mm) from the rim to leave space to add on additional toppings. If you overfill the tart, use an offset spatula to scrape off the excess and smooth out the filling.

4. Now it's time to finish your tart. You could cover it with fresh or roasted fruits or nuts. See page 310 for My Tips for Decoration. Finish the tart as desired and let the finishing set, if necessary.*

> * *If you use cut fruit, it's important to top off your tart with a coat of glaze or nappage (see page 223 for instructions). Not only is it more elegant, but it will also help prevent the fruit from drying out.*

5. When your tart is fully assembled and you're ready to dig in, use a serrated knife to slice the tart. Cut with a gentle sawing motion, rather than pressing down, to avoid crushing or breaking the sides of the tart shell.

Here are some additional tips to help you become a tart expert.

> **Be picky with your tart shell:** Make sure your tart shell is properly blind baked (see page 5)—lightly golden brown throughout without wet spots—and properly cooled, so it doesn't become too delicate to handle.

> **Use almond frangipane as a seal:** Before you blind bake your tart shell, you can add a thin layer of almond frangipane over the dough to help keep the filling from making the tart shell soggy. This is particularly useful if you plan to use a filling that's a bit watery or if you'll be packing up the tart and taking it elsewhere.

> **Add a little extra:** You can add a second layer of filling, like a thin layer of cake or jam, for extra flavor and texture. Assembling a tart doesn't need to be a one-filling situation. As a rule of thumb, just add the heavier filling first to the bottom of the shell so it doesn't sink. I'd put jam on the base and pastry cream on the top.

TRIPLE CHOCOLATE CAKE
BASE: Chocolate Cake (page 22)
FILLING: Dark Chocolate Ganache (page 137)
FINISHING: Chocolate Buttercream (page 222) + Cocoa Powder
TECHNIQUE: How to Assemble a Layer Cake (page 293)

HOW TO ASSEMBLE A LAYER CAKE

It's time to build your cake! Lopsided cakes are often a cause of fear, and I've heard plenty of tricks on how to get even layers, from placing toothpicks around the outside of the cake as markers to laying two flat bars on each side to using dental floss to slice the cake. I think it just takes practice, but practice doing it the right way. Skip the tricks.

Before you begin, make sure you have your cake and filling ready to go. If you would like to frost your cake immediately (I recommend this), prepare the finishing component (i.e., your glaze or buttercream) in advance.

YOU'LL NEED

1 cake (see Bases, page 20), unmolded
Filling of your choice (pages 121–208)*
Finishing(s) of your choice (pages 220–274)
Rotating cake stand or cake board (optional)
Serrated knife
Piping bag

> * For a thin layer of filling, you'll need about 250 grams (½ cup) filling; for a thicker layer, use 500 grams (1 cup).

1. After you unmold your cake, refrigerate it for about 15 minutes, until chilled. This makes the cake a bit firmer and therefore easier to slice. (A cake that's just out of the oven will be much more fragile.)

2. Place the chilled cake on a flat plate, cake board* or on a rotating cake stand. If the top of the cake is domed, set it domed-side up.

> * I like to use a cake board because it makes transferring the cake from one place to another much easier.

3. Now it's time to level and torte (this just means cutting it into layers). First decide how thick you'd like your layers, or if you'll be making a two- or three-layer cake. You should be able to cut one cake into three ½- to ¾-inch-thick (1.5 to 2 cm) layers* or two 1-inch-thick (2.5 cm) layers. The exact thickness of the layers is less important than that they be even.

> * I prefer ½- to ¾-inch-thick (1.5 to 2 cm) layers (that's on the thin side). However, if you're new to assembling cakes, you may feel more comfortable cutting thicker layers.

4. If the top of the cake is domed, use a serrated knife* to level it as best you can to ensure that the layers will be even. If your cake is thin and trimming off the top would mean you won't be able to cut the number of layers you need, you can just flip the domed layer upside down when you're assembling the cake so the flat side is up. It's better to trim off too little than too much.

      * *Serrated knives cut cakes and breads more delicately.*

5. Using the tip of a serrated knife, slowly score the lines where you will slice your cake in half, horizontally.*

      * *A rotating cake stand can help you cut even layers as you can simply turn the cake stand when you score.*

6. Starting with the bottom layer, use a sawing motion to slice along the scored line, increasing the depth of the cut as you go around the cake until you've cut all the way through the center. Gently lift off this first layer and set it on a cutting board. Repeat to divide the cake into two additional layers.

7. If you're not adding the filling right away, wrap each cake layer tightly in plastic wrap and store it at room temperature if you will be using the cake later that same day. Otherwise refrigerate it.*

      * *Sometimes, right before I assemble a cake, I use a small pastry brush to soak the layers with a bit of simple syrup or flavored syrup (see page 9) to keep them moist. This is a good technique to keep in your back pocket.*

8. When you're ready to fill the cake, start with the bottom layer of the cake because it is the most flat.

9. Temper your filling so it is soft and spreadable by mixing it with a spatula. Transfer your filling to a piping bag and snip off the tip to create a roughly ½-inch (1.5 cm) opening.*

      * *I prefer using a piping bag rather than an offset spatula to fill the cake layers, as it gives you a much cleaner finish.*

10. Gently pipe a ring of the filling around the edge of the first cake layer. This will act as a dam to hold in the rest of the filling. Pipe additional filling into the ring, covering the layer's surface.

11. Using both hands, gently lift the second layer of the cake and set it on top of the filling. Very gently press down on the top of the cake. (It's okay if a bit of the filling overflows at the sides; you can always clean it up as you're frosting the cake.)

12. If you're making a three-layer cake, pipe the filling on top as you did in step 10, then top with the final cake layer.*

      * *If the last layer is a bit domed, simply flip it so the flat side is facing up.*

13. If you're not frosting or otherwise finishing your cake right away, wrap it tightly in plastic wrap and refrigerate for up to 1 day; any longer and the cake may get dry.

14. Frost your cake as directed (see page 297), or see page 306 for instructions on glazing it (which will require an extra step).

HOW TO FROST A CAKE

In my opinion, a cake isn't truly finished until it's properly covered. Not only is the covering the final touch of decoration, but it also helps keep the cake moist. Whether the covering is buttercream, ganache, or meringue, it adds something. Frosting a cake takes a bit of practice, but it becomes much easier with the proper equipment. Set yourself up for success, and success will definitely be in reach.

YOU'LL NEED

Assembled cake (page 293)

Buttercream (pages 220–222), ganache (pages 137–144), or
   meringue (pages 258–265)*

Rotating cake stand

Large offset spatula

Bench scraper (optional, but recommended)

* *Some things to consider when choosing your frosting: Buttercream and ganache are the most stable; meringue and whipped ganache are lighter and don't last long. I don't recommend using Chantilly cream as a frosting, as it's too fragile.*

1. Place the cake on top of a cake board and in the center of a rotating cake stand* (if it isn't on one already).

* *Some cooks recommend putting a dab of buttercream or ganache in the center of the cake stand to keep the cake from sliding as you frost it. But I don't see the need—the ample weight of the cake should hold it in place.*

2. The first step to frosting a cake is to apply a crumb coat, a thin layer of frosting that holds any loose crumbs in place so they don't mar the surface of the final layer of frosting. Use an offset spatula to spread a thin layer of frosting over the entire cake. This layer doesn't have to be perfect; it's just a base coat. Refrigerate the cake for about 30 minutes, until the crumb coat is set.

3. Remove the cake from the refrigerator and return it to the cake stand. With the offset spatula, place a large dollop of the frosting* (about the size of a large grapefruit) at the center of the top of the cake.

* *Don't be afraid to put on too much frosting. You can always scrape it off.*

4. Hold the spatula at a 45-degree angle with the tip placed at the center of the cake and turn the cake stand slowly to spread the frosting.* A lot of extra frosting will go over the edge of the cake. This is what you want. Stop periodically to scrape the excess frosting on your spatula back into the bowl with the rest of the frosting.

* *Try to hold the offset spatula stationary as you rotate the cake stand for a smoother finish. If you don't have a rotating cake stand, just slowly turn the cake by hand.*

5. After frosting the top of the cake, use the excess frosting on the edges to cover the sides of the cake. Again, hold your spatula* stationary and at a 45-degree angle to the surface of the cake and turn the cake stand to spread the frosting. If you don't have enough frosting to cover the sides, add some more using your offset spatula, but you want to avoid doing this too much to make sure the cake has a clean finish. The less you touch it, the better it'll look.

* *I often prefer to use a bench scraper to spread the frosting at this point, as it's easier to hold along the sides of the cake.*

6. At this point you'll have just a tiny bit of excess frosting at the top rim of the cake. Use the offset spatula to smooth that out—try to do it in one swift movement.

7. Hold the spatula so just the tip is against the bottom edge of the cake and turn the cake stand to clean off any excess frosting. Voilà—you have frosted your cake!

8. Use the spatula to help you lift the cake off the stand (again, if you have a cake board, it can help tremendously here). You're ready to put the cake on a serving plate or refrigerate it until ready to serve.

HOW TO ASSEMBLE A MOUSSE CAKE

Once you've mastered a standard layer cake, try a mousse cake. Most of the European cakes that I was trained to make in culinary school fall into this category. Unlike a typical layer cake—which is built like a sandwich, with the cake layers as the "bread" and the filling in the middle—mousse cakes are constructed with a different logic. Before a mousse is chilled, it's liquid and pourable, so you can't just spread it over a cake layer. Instead, the mousse is poured straight on top of the cake base and around the layers of cake in between, if there are any, almost like a cast, and is then frozen. Once the mousse is set, you unmold it and let it come to room temperature. The resulting mousse cake is ethereally light, less sweet, and more finessed, with perfect angles and a completely flat top.

Here's how to get there.

LAYERED MOUSSE CAKE

In this book, a "layered mousse cake" consists of layers of cake, a mousse, and a finishing and is built in a round cake ring. Before you start assembling your mousse cake, make sure the cake base or cake layers and gelée (if you're using one) are ready to go.

YOU'LL NEED

Cake

Mousse of your choice (pages 190–205)*

Finishing(s) of your choice (pages 220–270)*

Serrated knife

8-inch (20 cm) cake ring with at least 2-inch (5 cm) sides

Offset spatula (optional, but recommended)

Acetate sheet or silicone baking mat

* Have the cake layers cut and the pan prepped before you prepare the mousse.

* I recommend finishing mousse cakes with a glaze. Mousse cakes can also be frosted with buttercream or ganache, but this is less conventional.

MATCHA PASSION FRUIT MOUSSE CAKE
BASE: Almond Cake (page 34)
FILLING: Matcha Mousse (page 192) + Passion Fruit Curd (page 136)
FINISHING: White Chocolate Glaze (page 234)
TECHNIQUE: How to Assemble a Mousse Cake (page 299)

1. After you unmold the cake, refrigerate it for 20 minutes, until chilled.* Cut the chilled cake into two or three layers (see page 293). Measure the size of the ring and make sure the cake is about ¼ inch (6 mm) smaller than the diameter of the cake ring. Use the cake ring as a guide to help you cut the cake, but it is okay if it is slightly uneven.

 * *A chilled cake is much easier to slice.*

2. Line a sheet pan with acetate or a silicone baking mat. Place an 8-inch (20 cm) cake ring on top of the pan. Cut a strip of acetate that's 26 inches (66 cm) long and slightly wider than the desired height of the finished mousse cake.* Line the cake ring with the acetate strip, overlapping the ends.

 * *The acetate will allow you to easily unmold the cake once it's set. If the cake ring is shorter than the desired height of the finished cake, you can cut the acetate strip a few inches wider to accommodate the height of the cake.*

3. When you have the cake layers ready and the cake ring prepared, make the mousse, then immediately begin to build the cake.

4. Pour a layer of mousse about ½ inch (1.5 cm) thick into the cake ring,* making sure there are no air bubbles. To get rid of air bubbles, lightly tap the sheet pan that the cake is sitting on and the air bubbles will rise to the top and pop. Use an offset spatula to level the mousse.*

 * *Mousse cakes are assembled upside down, so the ingredient at the bottom of the cake ring will be the top of the cake.*

 * *If you don't have an offset spatula, I've found that the back of spoon works well to push the mousse where it needs to go.*

5. Carefully set a layer of the cake on top of the mousse and gently press the cake into the mousse until the mousse comes over the edge of the cake a bit. (This ensures there are no bubbles.)

6. Pour another ½-inch-thick (1.5 cm) layer of mousse into the cake ring, covering the cake layer. Top with another cake layer—this will be the bottom of the cake. (If you have three cake layers, add another ½-inch-thick or 1.5 cm layer of mousse, then the final cake layer.)

7. Place the sheet pan in the freezer and freeze the mousse cake until frozen solid, about 3 hours or up to overnight.

8. At least 3 hours before serving, unmold the cake: Flip the cake ring so the cake layer is at the bottom and place the cake on a plastic 1-quart (1-liter) container. Gently push down on the cake ring to remove it, then transfer the cake to a cake board and remove the acetate strip.

9. Working quickly, while the cake is still frozen, glaze it* or finish it as desired, then return it to the freezer uncovered.

> * *If you're glazing the mousse cake, it must be frozen or it will melt from the heat of the glaze. And if it sits out on the counter and starts developing condensation, the glaze will weep.*

10. At least 2 hours before serving, transfer the cake to the refrigerator and let thaw completely. It can also be kept refrigerated for 1 to 2 days.

MOLDED MOUSSE CAKE

In a molded mousse cake, there is a much higher ratio of mousse to cake (just one layer of cake is used), so I recommend incorporating a gelée for extra flavor.

YOU'LL NEED
1 cake layer (see Bases page 20)
1 disc gelée of your choice (pages 168–172)
Mousse of your choice (pages 190–205)
Glaze of your choice (pages 223–234)*
Serrated knife
Silicone cake mold*
Offset spatula (recommended, but optional)

> * *I do not recommend frosting molded mousse cakes, as the shape of the mold can make the cake difficult to frost.*

> * *Molds are available in all shapes and sizes, ranging from simple domes and cubes to elaborate flowers and castles.*

1. Trim the cake layer and the disc of gelée so both are about ¼ inch (6 mm) smaller than the cake mold on all sides.

2. When you have the cake layer and gelée ready, make the mousse, then immediately begin to build the cake.

3. Pour half the mousse into the mold. Top it with the gelée and press down on the gelée gently but firmly to make sure there are no air bubbles in the mousse.*

  ∗ *You can also tap the mold lightly against the counter to force out any bubbles.*

4. Pour in the remaining mousse, then top the mousse with the layer of cake (this will be the bottom of the cake). Gently press down on the cake.

5. Freeze the mousse cake until frozen solid, about 3 hours or up to overnight.

6. At least 3 hours before serving, take the cake out of the freezer and unmold it. If you are not glazing it immediately, wrap it tightly in plastic wrap and return it to the freezer.

7. Working quickly, while the cake is still frozen, glaze it, then return it to the freezer uncovered.*

  ∗ *The cake must be frozen when you glaze it, or it will melt from the heat of the glaze. And if the cake sits out on the counter and starts developing condensation, the glaze will weep.*

8. At least 2 hours before serving, transfer the cake to the refrigerator and let thaw completely. It can also be kept refrigerated for 1 to 2 days.

HOW TO GLAZE A CAKE

A neatly glazed cake is like a perfectly tailored suit—timeless and sophisticated. But a glaze also does little to hide any flaws in the cake beneath it, so make sure you have a neatly trimmed cake or smooth mousse (without any bubbles).

Glazing is perhaps the most advanced finishing method because mistakes are obvious. The key to perfectly glazing a cake is twofold. The first is to master a flow. Do each step in one fell swoop and do not hesitate. Have everything ready to go, and you will not need to fix the glaze—trying to fix it will often make it look worse.

The second is to make sure you are controlling temperatures. Glazes need to be warm when they hit cold surfaces.

Before you start, make sure you have the cake fully assembled and ready for the finishing.

> If it's a mousse cake, keep the cake frozen until just before you glaze it. Otherwise, the glaze will melt the mousse.

> If it's an unfrosted ("naked") regular cake, refrigerate the cake until cold before glazing it. A chilled cake won't absorb the glaze. I would usually do this for a loaf cake.

> An unfrosted regular cake can also be crumb coated (see page 297) with ganache, then frozen for 4 hours or overnight before glazing. The glaze goes on much smoother this way.

> A cake frosted with buttercream or any finishing other than ganache cannot be glazed—the glaze will not stick to the finishing.

YOU'LL NEED

An assembled cake

Glaze of your choice (pages 223–234)

Digital thermometer (optional)

Large offset spatula (optional, but recommended)

1. If the glaze is freshly prepared, make sure it's hot. If it has cooled or if you prepared the glaze in advance, transfer it to a microwave-safe bowl or a plastic 1-quart (1-liter) container* and microwave until the glaze is hot (but not so hot that it will burn your fingertips if you touch it) and pourable, about 30 seconds. If you have a thermometer handy, you can heat the glaze to exactly to 113° to 122°F or 45° to 50°C. Do not overheat the glaze, or it will turn dull. Add a little water to loosen it up if it's too thick. If the glaze has separated, blend it using a hand blender for a few seconds to combine, then tap the container on the counter once or twice to remove any air bubbles that may have formed during blending.*

> * *A plastic quart container is a great way to pour glaze over a cake; you can pinch the container slightly to form a makeshift spout, which allows you to pour with more accuracy.*
>
> * *Make sure there are no air bubbles in the glaze, or they'll be transferred onto the cake.*

2. Set a wire rack over a rimmed sheet pan. Take the cake out of the refrigerator or freezer, unwrap it if necessary, and set it on the rack.

3. Pour the glaze generously and quickly into the center of the top of the cake, without hesitation. It should pool and spread outward from the center on its own. Do not pour it around the edges of the cake or from side to side, as this will cause it to set unevenly and form ripples in the glaze. Continue pouring until the glaze has fully coated the sides of the cake.

4. If you are glazing a flat cake, run a large offset spatula over the top of the cake in one smooth stroke—again, without hesitation—to remove excess glaze.

5. Transfer the glazed cake to the refrigerator and let thaw for at least 4 hours before serving. (Do not thaw mousse cakes at room temperature, or they will melt.)

HOW TO GLAZE A TART

I recommend finishing tarts with nappage or another glaze. The basic technique is similar to that for glazing a cake.

YOU'LL NEED
An assembled tart
Glaze of your choice (pages 223–234)
Digital thermometer (optional)
Pastry brush (optional, for brushing nappage over fruit-topped tarts)

1. Prep the glaze as directed in step 1 of "How to Glaze a Cake (page 306)."

2. Set a wire rack over a rimmed sheet pan and set the tart on the rack.

3. To finish the tart with a flat, even layer of glaze, pour the glaze generously and quickly into the direct center of the top of the tart, without hesitation. It should pool and spread outward from the center on its own. Do not pour it from side to side, as this will cause it to set unevenly and form ripples in the glaze. Continue pouring until the whole tart is covered; use a pastry brush to lightly brush a thin layer of glaze to cover fruits completely.

4. Pick up the wire rack and tap lightly onto the sheet tray to remove any excess glaze. Then let slightly set for 1 minute. Don't touch it! Further touching will only mess up the tart.

MY TIPS FOR DECORATIONS

Sometimes that final "cherry on top" is the most crucial part of all. After all the effort you've put into building each component of your cake or tart, you don't want to neglect the finishing touches. There are really no rules as to how to do it properly. It's time to express your own style! Here are some of my tips for getting started.

What's in the cake should be on top of it: One of my biggest pet peeves is when an ingredient that's not in the cake is used as decoration on top of it. Finishing components are a clue for what flavors are hidden on the inside.

Simpler is always better: It's like the old adage from Coco Chanel about not overaccessorizing. A rookie mistake is trying to do too much rather than confidently standing behind one vision and style. Better to have just a pristine, beautifully glazed cake with just a sprinkling of sea salt than to cover it up with a clutter of nuts, chocolate, and fruits.

Off center: When decorating your cake, look toward the edges first rather than plopping everything in the center. It's often the subtle adornment in the corner or around the sides that is more visually effective than an in-your-face cake topping. Remember, your decorations are a supporting character; the cake is the hero.

Uniformity: When working with fruit, it's about generosity and repetition. As a general rule, you're always looking out for two things: the same size, facing the same direction. Try to place fruits as close as possible, and even overlapping, to hide the filling underneath.

Keep it edible: Garnishing cakes with candied pearls, leaves, or even decorative paper isn't quite my style. For me, a decoration should be edible. Flavor wins over looks any day.

Do things with intent: Even if you're just adding a tiny sprinkle of sea salt, decorate with intent. Sprinkle sea salt with your fingertips in a straight line or design of your choice. Don't just scatter it across the surface of the cake or tart. If you are dusting something with confectioners' sugar, think about whether you want to dust just along the edges, or on an angle (in which case you can use a piece of paper as a stencil). Every bit of extra effort and care will show.

USING A PIPING BAG

Piping bags are a small step up, but they're one of my favorite tools that's easily affordable and widely available. Once you bring them into your repertoire, you'll wonder how you ever lived without them.

SELECTING A PIPING TIP

There are three types of tips I recommend:

> **At the very least: Plain Tips**—Plain tips are great for piping ladyfingers, macarons, and a wide variety of designs—lines, spheres, and teardrops. A plain tip can also be used for filling anything from éclairs to cream puffs. (As a trick, I sometimes use them to remove the pits from cherries once I cut off both sides.)

> **A bit more prepared: Star Tips**—Star tips are my preferred choice for piping choux dough. They create ridges that allow the steam inside the choux to escape so there are no large cracks on the surface, which can happen if you use a plain tip.

> **Upgrade: Saint-Honoré Tips**—A Saint-Honoré tip is my favorite "fancy" tip and is used mostly for decorating. Named after the classic French cake with a chevron piping design, it looks like a standard round tip but with a V-shaped cutout in one side. This cut side should always be facing up as you pipe.

Like golf clubs, there's a specific size tip for each task, but I find that my go-to is a tip with a ⅜-inch-diameter (1 cm) opening, as it is large enough for piping choux and cake, but still can be small enough for most cake decorations. In more advanced cake decorating, you may want to use more than one tip with the same frosting. This is easy to do with a tip coupler, a plastic insert with a screw-on ring. Instead of putting the piping tip directly into the bag, you unscrew the ring around the coupler insert, put the insert into the bag, and snip off the tip of the bag. Then you can put a piping tip on the coupler insert and screw on the ring to hold the tip in place. This allows you to switch the tip easily without having to use multiple piping bags.

And you don't *always* need a piping tip. Cutting off the tip of the piping bag can suffice if you're not doing anything intricate. I often use just the piping bag sans tip when working with looser fillings such as pastry cream or mousses, as it's easier than using a spatula to fill a cake or tart shell.

HOW TO FILL A PIPING BAG

After selecting your tip (if you're using one), it's time fill the piping bag.

1. Place the piping tip in the bag narrow-side down and push it down to the tip of the bag. Cut off the tip of the piping bag so the opening is large enough that the piping tip is exposed. (Do this before filling your bag; after, it will be too late.)

2. Take some loose slack of the piping bag and shove it into the tip so that it prevents things from leaking once you start filling.

3. Using your nondominant hand, form an open C shape with your thumb and index finger around roughly the middle of the piping bag and fold the top of the bag down over your hand. This keeps the piping bag open so it's easy to fill. You can also use a quart container to hold the bag open by folding it over the sides of the container.

4. Using your other hand, use a spatula to scoop the filling into the bag. The key is to NEVER OVERFILL. Do not fill your piping bag more than midway. You can always refill.

5. Once you reach that halfway point, twist the bag where the filling stops and push the filling toward the tip.

HOW TO PIPE

Proper piping takes practice—you need to work on three things: the distance you hold the tip from the surface onto which you're piping, the pressure you apply to the piping bag, and the final pull away.

1. Hold the piping page in the palm of your dominant hand. The filling should fit almost entirely in your palm; this will give you the most control. Use your other hand to guide the bag. Twist the top of the piping bag to make sure it is held closed and your filling doesn't get squeezed out on the back end.

2. In general, hold the tip close to the surface onto which you are piping; this will lead to the most accurate results. Depending on the shape you are piping, you may choose to hold the tip at a 90-degree angle to the surface (if you're piping a ball of choux for cream puffs or a teardrop shape for decoration, for example) or a 45-degree angle to the surface (if you're piping éclairs or a line of frosting for decoration, for example).

3. Hold the bag firmly and use the palm and base of your thumb to gently squeeze.

4. As you near the end of the piping, release the pressure on the bag completely and pull the tip away from the surface in one swift motion. The direction in which you pull will leave a small "tail," so pull away toward where there is the most dough or cream piped. For instance, if you are piping a circle, twist your wrist at the last minute so the tail spirals inward. If you are piping an éclair, pull back toward the body of the éclair so the tail merges with the body and doesn't stick out at the end.

5. Once you are done piping, cleanup is easy. Squeeze any extra filling or frosting into an airtight container (or back into its original container) and store for later use according to the storage instructions in the recipe. Use scissors to cut the piping bag above the tip, then remove and wash the tip. Discard the piping bag. If you are using a reusable piping bag, invert the bag and wash thoroughly and dry with a towel first before leaving it out to dry fully.

A Cake Is a Gift

In our bakeries around the world, we have open kitchens. Our work happens on the floor with only clear windows as barriers between us and the guests. Everything we do, they can see. Through one window, they may see slabs of croissant dough, ready to roll through a dough sheeter, becoming thinner with each pass; through another, chocolate chip cookies are cooling from the oven on a speed rack and the smell is passing through the entire shop; and look, there—a cook is piping raspberry jam into fresh raspberries before placing them on a tart. The kids press their faces against the glass as they watch, giggling, and our chefs often look up to wave.

But we didn't build open kitchens simply to entertain our guests. The transparent glass works both ways—we're also looking at you. I, for one, am always taking a peek to see how our guests eat. Do they pick up the pastry with their hands? How quickly do they take the second bite after the first? Do they talk about it in between the bites? And of course—is their plate clean when they leave?

Above all, the thing that tells me the success of a dessert is the number of smiles it generates. Even when I worked at Restaurant Daniel many years ago, I would linger for just a moment at the table after bringing a slice of my plated chocolate hazelnut cake to guests. I wanted to see their reaction. No written review or number of stars made a difference to me if the first bite of dessert was met with stern faces.

We order desserts not because we have to, but because we want to. Desserts are playful, and, most important, they demand that you play along. Cakes are often central to traditions. In France, on the festival of the Epiphany at the end of the Christmas season, we serve king's cake with a small favor called a *fève* (French for "fava bean") hidden inside; whoever finds it becomes king for the day. When I moved to the US, I learned that couples save the top tier of their wedding cake to eat on their first anniversary.

My favorite ritual, however, is the simplest one—I love lighting birthday candles. A birthday candle gives a cake magical powers: it can grant wishes. There's that moment of silence when the birthday girl or boy closes their eyes to make a wish and everyone eagerly waits, holding their breath. A deep inhale, and then darkness as the smoke slowly rises, bringing our hopes and dreams up toward the sky.

I've done my homework on this ritual. Some believe it grew from an ancient Greek tradition of offering cakes to Artemis, goddess of the moon, where the candle flames represented the glow of the moonlight. Others say the candles scare away evil spirits and offer protection to people crossing the bridge into another year of life. A friend of mine swears it's a marketing ploy to sell more candles. But the purpose of my research wasn't just to understand the origins of this ritual. I wanted to know if there was any truth behind the magic that adults tell us about. What, I wondered, were the chances a wish would be granted?

Growing up, I often wished for the same thing on my birthday: I wished for a future where I would leave France to travel around the world, exploring new places. And added to that—it wouldn't hurt if I could eat a bit more cake along the way. I closed my eyes, pressed my palms together, and wished.

Cake is not for sustenance, but for celebration. It's something extra; it's a gift; it's for your heart, not your stomach. No appetizer or entrée could ever do the same. That's why I do what I do. That's why I love to bake. As for wishes being granted by blowing out a birthday candle? I am and forever will be a believer.

ACKNOWLEDGMENTS

I'd like to thank:

Jessica, who always cares (about big things and small things, and all that's in between).

Fitz, who always finds time to do more (amidst long hours and hard days and even harder holidays).

Michael, and Michael's mom, Leona (who made a chocolate cherry cake using these recipes).

Many thanks, too, to my editor, Emily; our recipe tester, Samantha; and our photographer, Evan; who made every image look delicious.

And to my teams around the world, thank you for believing in how much joy a simple pastry can bring.

INDEX

Page numbers in *italics* refer to photo captions.

ABOUT THE AUTHOR

DOMINIQUE ANSEL, a James Beard Award–winning pastry chef, has shaken up the pastry world with innovation and creativity at the heart of his work. As chef and owner of eponymous bakeries in New York, London, and Los Angeles, Chef Dominique has been responsible for creating some of the most fêted pastries in the world, including: the Cronut® (named one of *TIME* magazine's "25 Best Inventions of 2013"), the Cookie Shot, Frozen S'more, Blossoming Hot Chocolate, and many more.

For his prolific creativity, he was named the World's Best Pastry Chef in 2017 by the World's 50 Best Restaurants awards. *Food & Wine* has called him a "Culinary Van Gogh" while the *New York Post* coined him "the Willy Wonka of New York." He was also named one of *Business Insider*'s "Most Innovative People Under 40," one of *Crain*'s "40 Under 40," and was bestowed the prestigious L'ordre du Mérite Agricole, France's second-highest honor. Dominique's first cookbook, *Dominique Ansel: The Secret Recipes*, was published in 2014.

Prior to opening his own shop, Dominique served as the executive pastry chef for the restaurant Daniel, when the team earned its coveted third Michelin star and a four-star review from the *New York Times*. He opened his first bakery in NYC's SoHo neighborhood in 2011 with just four employees.